DR. GORDON L. BOGGS

UNDERSTANDING THE BOOK OF REVELATION

WHAT DOES THE BIBLE SAY?

WestBow
PRESS®
A DIVISION OF THOMAS NELSON
& ZONDERVAN

Copyright © 2019 Dr. Gordon L. Boggs.

All rights reserved. No part of this book may be used or reproduced by any means, graphic, electronic, or mechanical, including photocopying, recording, taping or by any information storage retrieval system without the written permission of the author except in the case of brief quotations embodied in critical articles and reviews.

WestBow Press books may be ordered through booksellers or by contacting:

WestBow Press
A Division of Thomas Nelson & Zondervan
1663 Liberty Drive
Bloomington, IN 47403
www.westbowpress.com
1 (866) 928-1240

Because of the dynamic nature of the Internet, any web addresses or links contained in this book may have changed since publication and may no longer be valid. The views expressed in this work are solely those of the author and do not necessarily reflect the views of the publisher, and the publisher hereby disclaims any responsibility for them.

Any people depicted in stock imagery provided by Getty Images are models, and such images are being used for illustrative purposes only.
Certain stock imagery © Getty Images.

Scripture taken from the King James Version of the Bible.

Scripture taken from the New King James Version®. Copyright © 1982 by Thomas Nelson. Used by permission. All rights reserved.

ISBN: 978-1-9736-5022-5 (sc)
ISBN: 978-1-9736-5021-8 (hc)
ISBN: 978-1-9736-5023-2 (e)

Library of Congress Control Number: 2019900098

Print information available on the last page.

WestBow Press rev. date: 2/22/2019

CONTENTS

CHAPTER 1	God Wants Us to Understand	1
CHAPTER 2	Jesus Wants Us to Understand	27
CHAPTER 3	The Holy Spirit Wants Us to Understand	49
CHAPTER 4	Understanding the Final Seven Years—Part 1	69
CHAPTER 5	Understanding the Final Seven Years—Part 2	87
CHAPTER 6	Understanding the Seventh Trumpet and the Summary of Revelation 12:1–14:20	101
CHAPTER 7	Understanding the Seven Bowls of the Wrath of God	117
CHAPTER 8	Understanding the Biblical Sequence of Events	143

CHAPTER 1

God Wants Us to Understand

The Book of Revelation has been a mystery to many people for many years.

One of the basic roadblocks to understanding the Book of Revelation has been the fact that there is no Temple in Jerusalem. The Temple in Jerusalem had been destroyed in AD 70 just as Jesus had prophesied thirty-seven years earlier as recorded in Matthew 24:1–2.

> Then Jesus went out and departed from the Temple, and His disciples came up to show Him the buildings of the Temple. And Jesus said to them, "Do you not see all these things? Assuredly, I say to you, not one stone shall be left here upon another, that shall not be thrown down."

When the armies of the Roman Empire under the leadership of Titus destroyed the Temple in AD 70, it was set on fire and the soldiers tore it apart stone by stone to get to the melted gold. Both the Temple and Jerusalem were destroyed and not one stone was left upon another as Jesus had prophesied.

For the next nineteen hundred–plus years, and for almost two thousand years since the Book of Revelation was written, there has been no Temple in Jerusalem! Nevertheless, when John, the author of Revelation, was shown these coming end-time events, he was instructed to measure the Temple and those who worship there as recorded in Revelation 11:1–8.

> Then I was given a reed like a measuring rod. And the angel stood, saying, "Rise and measure the Temple of God, the altar, and those who worship there. But leave out the court which is outside the Temple, and do not measure it, for it has been given to the Gentiles. And they will tread the holy city underfoot for forty-two months [three and a half years]. And I will give power to my two witnesses [Two Prophets], and they will prophesy one thousand two hundred and sixty days [the same three and a half years], clothed in sackcloth."
>
> These are the two olive trees and the two lampstands standing before the God of the earth.
>
> And if anyone wants to harm them, fire proceeds from their mouth and devours their enemies. And if anyone wants to harm them, he must be killed in this manner. These [Two Prophets] have the power to shut heaven, so that no rain falls in the days of their prophecy; and they have power over waters to turn them to blood, and to strike the earth will all plagues, as often as they desire.
>
> When they finish their testimony, the beast that ascends out of the bottomless pit will make war against them, overcome them, and kill them. And their dead bodies will lie in the street of the great city which spiritually is called Sodom and Egypt, where also our Lord was crucified [Jerusalem].

The Temple was also mentioned in the prophecies of Jesus as He spoke with His disciples concerning these end-time events as recorded in Matthew 24:15–22.

> Therefore when you see the "Abomination of Desolation," [this event occurs inside the Temple] spoken of by Daniel the prophet, standing in the holy place [the Holy of Holies in the Temple]—whoever reads, let him understand—,

> then let those who are in Judea flee to the mountains. Let him who is on the housetop not go down to take anything out of his house. And let him who is in the field not go back to get his clothes. But woe to those who are pregnant and to those who are nursing babies in those days! And pray that your flight may not be in winter or on the Sabbath.
>
> For then there will be great Tribulation, such as has not been since the beginning of the world until this time, no, nor ever shall be. And unless those days were shortened, no flesh would be saved; but for the elect's sake those days will be shortened [An event will occur at the end of the Tribulation which will "shorten the days" of the Tribulation for the sake of the elect].

This is an amazing scripture because the disciple Matthew (who wrote the Gospel of Matthew) interrupted a prophetic message by Jesus and inserted—in parentheses—the phrase "Whoever reads, let him understand" and then completed the prophecy. It is as if Matthew is waving his arms to get our attention and saying, "This is important! You need to get this!"

Mark did the same thing in Mark 13:14–20.

> So when you see the "Abomination of Desolation", [this event occurs inside the Temple] spoken of by Daniel the prophet, standing where it ought not—let the reader understand—, then let those who are in Judea flee to the mountains. Let him who is on the housetop not go down into the house, nor enter to take anything out of his house. And let him who is in the field not go back to get his clothes. But woe to those who are pregnant and to those who are nursing babies in those days! And pray that your flight may not be in winter.
>
> For in those days there will be Tribulation, such as has not been since the beginning of the creation which God

created until this time, nor ever shall be. And unless the Lord had shortened those days, no flesh would be saved; but for the elect's sake, whom He chose, He shortened the days [The Lord will cause an event to occur at the end of the Tribulation which will "shorten the days" of the Tribulation for the sake of the elect whom the Lord chose].

So Matthew, an original disciple of Jesus, and Mark both understood what Jesus was teaching in regard to these end-time events. And when Jesus mentioned the "Abomination of Desolation" [which occurs inside the Temple], both of them inserted—in parentheses—the phrase "Whoever reads, let him understand" or the phrase "Let the reader understand". It is as if both of them are waving their arms to get our attention and saying, "This is important! You need to get this!"

Of course, it could be that Matthew and Mark were recording what Jesus actually said. If Jesus actually said—"Whoever reads, let him understand" or "Let the reader understand", then it becomes an even more significant statement! If that were the case, then it would be Jesus Himself telling us, "This is important! You need to get this!"

In either case, it is very important for us to understand the Biblical definition of the "Abomination of Desolation" [which occurs inside the Temple].

In discussing end-time events in 2 Thessalonians 2:1–5, Paul describes the "Abomination of Desolation" [which occurs inside the Temple] as an end-time event that will be committed by the coming "Antichrist".

> Now, brethren, concerning the coming of our Lord Jesus Christ and our gathering together to Him, we ask you not to be soon shaken in mind or troubled, either by spirit or by word or by letter, as if from us, as though the day of Christ had come.
>
> Let no one deceive you by any means; for that Day will not come unless the falling away comes first, and the man of sin [the Antichrist] is revealed, the son of perdition [the Antichrist], who opposes and exalts himself above all

that is called God or that is worshipped, so that he [the Antichrist] sits as God in the Temple of God, showing himself that he is God [This event is what the Bible refers to as the "Abomination of Desolation"].

Do you not remember that when I was still with you I told you these things?

In other words, the "Abomination of Desolation" occurs when the Antichrist goes into the Temple — in Jerusalem — into the Holy of Holies — and sits as God — in the Temple of God — and proclaims that he is God. This event is what the Bible refers to as the "Abomination of Desolation" and this event occurs inside the Temple.

It is also important to notice that Jesus mentioned a time that will come in the future which He referred to as the "Tribulation" in Matthew 24:15–22. Let's read that again and I will underline the word "Tribulation".

Therefore when you see the "Abomination of Desolation," [which occurs inside the Temple] spoken of by Daniel the prophet, standing in the holy place [This is the event where the Antichrist enters the Holy of Holies in the Temple in Jerusalem and sits as God in the Temple of God and proclaims that he is God. This event is what the Bible refers to as the "Abomination of Desolation"]—whoever reads, let him understand—, then let those who are in Judea flee to the mountains. Let him who is on the housetop not go down to take anything out of his house. And let him who is in the field not go back to get his clothes. But woe to those who are pregnant and to those who are nursing babies in those days! And pray that your flight may not be in winter or on the Sabbath.

For then there will be great <u>Tribulation</u>, such as has not been since the beginning of the world until this time, no, nor ever shall be. And unless those days were shortened, no flesh would be saved; but for the elect's sake those days will be shortened [An event will occur at the end of the Tribulation which will "shorten the days" of the Tribulation for the sake of the elect].

In Mark 13:14–20, Jesus said,

> So when you see the "Abomination of Desolation", [which occurs inside the Temple] spoken of by Daniel the prophet, standing where it ought not [This is the event where the Antichrist enters the Holy of Holies in the Temple in Jerusalem and sits as God in the Temple of God and proclaims that he is God. This event is what the Bible refers to as the "Abomination of Desolation"]—let the reader understand—, then let those who are in Judea flee to the mountains. Let him who is on the housetop not go down into the house, nor enter to take anything out of his house. And let him who is in the field not go back to get his clothes. But woe to those who are pregnant and to those who are nursing babies in those days! And pray that your flight may not be in winter.
>
> For in those days there will be <u>Tribulation</u>, such as has not been since the beginning of the creation which God created until this time, nor ever shall be. And unless the Lord had shortened those days, no flesh would be saved; but for the elect's sake, whom He chose, He shortened the days [The Lord will cause an event to occur at the end of the Tribulation which will "shorten the days" of the Tribulation for the sake of the elect whom the Lord chose].

In other words, Jesus is saying that toward the end of the Tribulation, it will be so bad that all His disciples would be killed unless He caused an event to occur that would "shorten the days" of the Tribulation. This event will actually end the Tribulation and we can see that event very clearly in Matthew 24:29–31. I will underline a few words so that we can "see" the biblical sequence of events.

> Immediately after the Tribulation of those days the sun will be darkened, and the moon will not give its light; the stars will fall from heaven, and the powers of the heavens will be shaken. Then the sign of the Son of Man will appear in heaven, and then all the tribes of the earth will mourn, and they will see the Son of Man coming on the clouds of Heaven with power and great glory. And He will send His angels with a great sound of a trumpet, and they will gather His elect from the four winds, from one end of heaven to the other [This event is known as the "Rapture"].

So the event that we read about in Matthew 24:15–22 where Jesus prophesied that an event will occur at the end of the Tribulation which will "shorten the days" of the Tribulation for the sake of the elect appears to be the exact same event that we see here in Matthew 24:29–31 where Jesus will send His angels with a great sound of a Trumpet and they will gather His elect from the four winds, from one end of heaven to the other. This event is known as the "Rapture".

Here is the way Mark records this. Again, I will underline a few words so that we can "see" the biblical sequence of events.

> But in those days, after that Tribulation, the sun will be darkened, and the moon will not give its light; the stars of heaven will fall, and the powers in the heavens will be shaken. Then they will see the Son of Man coming in the clouds with great power and glory. And then He will send His angels, and gather together His elect from the four winds, from the farthest part of the earth to the farthest part of heaven [This event is known as the "Rapture"]. (Mark 13:24–27)

So the event that we read about in Mark 13:14–20 where Jesus prophesied that the Lord will cause an event to occur at the end of the Tribulation which will "shorten the days" of the Tribulation for the sake of the elect whom the Lord chose appears to be the exact same event that we see here in Mark 13:24–27 where Jesus will send His angels, and gather together His elect from the four winds, from the farthest part of the earth to the farthest part of heaven. This event is known as the "Rapture".

Therefore, let's read this one more time, because this is the way that we should read and understand Matthew 24:15–22. Again, I will underline a few words to help us "see" the biblical sequence of events.

> Therefore when you see the "<u>Abomination of Desolation</u>," [which occurs inside the Temple] spoken of by Daniel the prophet, standing in the holy place [This is the event where the Antichrist enters the Holy of Holies in the Temple in Jerusalem and sits as God in the Temple of God and proclaims that he is God. This event is what the Bible refers to as the "Abomination of Desolation"]— whoever reads, let him understand—, <u>then</u> let those who are in Judea flee to the mountains. Let him who is on the housetop not go down to take anything out of his house. And let him who is in the field not go back to get his clothes. But woe to those who are pregnant and to those who are nursing babies in those days! And pray that your flight may not be in winter or on the Sabbath.
>
> <u>For then</u> there will be <u>great Tribulation, such as has not been since the beginning of the world until this time, no, nor ever shall be</u>. And unless those days were shortened, no flesh would be saved; but for the elect's sake those days will be shortened [An event will occur at the end of the Tribulation which will "shorten the days" of the Tribulation for the sake of the elect. This event appears to be the exact same event as described by Jesus in Matthew 24:29–31 where the Son of Man is seen coming on the clouds of heaven with power and great glory, where He will send His angels with a great sound of a trumpet, and where they gather His elect from the four winds, from one end of heaven to the other. This event is known as the "Rapture"].

Likewise, this is the way we should read and understand Mark 13:14–20. Again, I will underline a few words to help us "see" the biblical sequence of events.

> So when you see the "Abomination of Desolation", [which occurs inside the Temple] spoken of by Daniel the prophet, standing where it ought not [This is the event where the Antichrist enters the Holy of Holies in the Temple in Jerusalem and sits as God in the Temple of God and proclaims that he is God. This event is what the Bible refers to as the "Abomination of Desolation"]—let the reader understand—, then let those who are in Judea flee to the mountains. Let him who is on the housetop not go down into the house, nor enter to take anything out of his house. And let him who is in the field not go back to get his clothes. But woe to those who are pregnant and to those who are nursing babies in those days! And pray that your flight may not be in winter.
>
> For in those days there will be Tribulation, such as has not been since the beginning of the creation which God created until this time, nor ever shall be. And unless the Lord had shortened those days, no flesh would be saved; but for the elect's sake, whom He chose, He shortened the days [The Lord will cause an event to occur at the end of the Tribulation which will "shorten the days" of the Tribulation for the sake of the elect whom the Lord chose. This appears to be the exact same event as described by Jesus in Mark 13:24–27 where the Son of Man comes in the clouds with great power and glory, and where He sends His angels to gather His elect from the four winds, from the farthest part of earth to the farthest part of heaven. This event is known as the "Rapture"]

Many people have been taught that the Rapture occurs prior to the Tribulation and therefore many people have been taught that Christians do not go through the Tribulation. Nevertheless, in these passages of Scripture, Jesus is clearly teaching His disciples that the "Rapture" occurs <u>after</u> the "Tribulation".

In order to understand the Book of Revelation, it is important to understand the actual biblical sequence of events. Throughout this book, as we look at the actual biblical sequence of events and as we study "What Does the Bible Say?"—we will discover that the "Wrath of God" occurs <u>after</u> the "Rapture". The sequence of end-time events that the Bible teaches is this.

- Tribulation.
- Rapture.
- Wrath of God.

It is important to understand that there is a major difference between the <u>Tribulation</u> and the <u>Wrath of God</u>. Jesus commands that each of His disciples be "Faithful unto Death". Therefore when the disciples of Jesus obey the commandments of Jesus, they will be able to go through the <u>Tribulation</u> and "not stumble". In other words, when the disciples of Jesus obey the commandments of Jesus, they will be able to "Stand" and they will "Overcome" by the <u>Blood of the Lamb</u> and they will "Overcome" by the <u>Word of their Testimony</u> and they will "Overcome" because they will be "<u>Faithful unto Death</u>". Nevertheless, the Bible also teaches that Christians will <u>NOT</u> go through the <u>Wrath of God</u>.

In John 16:33, Jesus said, "These things I have spoken to you, that in Me you may have peace. In the world you will have Tribulation; but be of good cheer, I have overcome the world."

We will discuss the following in much more detail later in this book and give the actual scripture references, but in the Book of Revelation, when John saw Jesus take the Scroll from the hand of God, there were Seven Seals, and Seven Thunders, and Seven Trumpets, and Seven Bowls of Wrath. These Seven Bowls of Wrath are the <u>Wrath of God</u>. Therefore it is important to understand that there is a major difference between the <u>Tribulation</u> and the <u>Wrath of God</u>.

What we call the "<u>Seven-year Tribulation</u>" has to do with the Seven Seals, and the Seven Thunders, and the Seven Trumpets. What the Bible calls the "<u>Wrath of God</u>" has to do with the Seven Bowls of Wrath.

Throughout Scripture, the sequence of end-time events that the Bible teaches is this.

- Tribulation.
- Rapture.
- Wrath of God.

Again, we will discuss the following in much more detail later in this book and give the actual scripture references, but the Bible teaches that the Rapture occurs at the "Last Trumpet" [which we will see later is actually the last of the Seven Trumpets mentioned above]. Therefore, the disciples of Jesus will have endured everything prior to the Seventh Trumpet. This includes the entire seven-year period of Tribulation and Persecution and the destruction of basically one-half of the earth's population. We will also see later that the Bible teaches that the disciples of Jesus [who obey the commandments of Jesus] will be "Faithful unto Death" as they go through this time of Tribulation and Persecution. We will also see later that after the Two Prophets are killed, the Antichrist will go into the Temple — in Jerusalem — into the Holy of Holies — and sit as God — in the Temple of God — and proclaim that he [the Antichrist] is God. This event is what the Bible refers to as the "Abomination of Desolation". After the "Abomination of Desolation" has occurred, the Antichrist will begin a period that Jesus refers to as the "Great Tribulation" [where it has never been that bad before and where it will never be that bad again]. Then prior to all of His disciples being killed, Jesus will implement the event that we call the "Rapture". The event that the Bible calls the "Wrath of God" will follow the event of the "Rapture", but the disciples of Jesus will certainly <u>NOT</u> go through the <u>Wrath of God</u>.

The Bible teaches that the Seven Bowls of Wrath [Wrath of God] occur <u>after</u> the "Rapture". The Bible teaches that the Seven Bowls of Wrath [Wrath of God] are poured out onto an unsaved world. The Bible teaches that the disciples of Jesus do <u>NOT</u> go through the <u>Wrath of God</u>. Instead, the Bible teaches in Ephesians that the "Wrath of God" is poured out upon the "sons of disobedience". Again, I will underline a few words.

> Let no one deceive you with empty words, for because of these things the Wrath of God [Wrath of God] comes upon the <u>sons of disobedience</u>. (Ephesians 5:6)

Paul makes the point that at one time we were all "sons of disobedience". But when a person does what the Bible says that they have to do in order to be "saved", then that person becomes alive with Christ and is "born again". Look at Ephesians 2:1-10:

> And you He made alive, who were dead in trespasses and sins, in which you once walked according to the course of this world, according to the prince of the power of the air [Satan], the spirit who now works in the <u>sons of disobedience</u>, among whom also we all once conducted ourselves in the lusts of our flesh, fulfilling the desires of the flesh and of the mind and were by nature children of <u>wrath</u>, just as the others.
>
> But God, who is rich in mercy, because of His great love with which He loved us, even when we were dead in trespasses, made us alive together with Christ (by grace you have been saved), and raised us up together in the heavenly places in Christ Jesus. For by grace you have been saved through faith, and that not of yourselves; it is the gift of God, not of works, lest anyone should boast. For we are His workmanship, created in Christ Jesus for good works, which God prepared beforehand that we should walk in them.

When people are taught that Christians do not go through the Tribulation, most of the Bible verses that they are shown actually have the word *wrath* in them. The Bible teaches that Christians do not go through **wrath** [Christians do <u>NOT</u> go through the <u>Wrath of God</u>], but many people have used those exact same verses to teach people that Christians do not go through Tribulation. In 1 Thessalonians 5:9-10, Paul wrote, "For God did not appoint us to **wrath** [God did <u>NOT</u> appoint us to the <u>Wrath of God</u>], but to obtain salvation through our Lord Jesus Christ, who died for us, that whether we wake or sleep, we should live together with Him." This simply means that Christians do <u>NOT</u> go through the <u>Wrath of God</u>.

There are many similar Scriptures, but look at Romans 5:9, "Much more then, having now been justified by His blood, we shall be saved from **wrath** [We shall be saved from the Wrath of God] through Him." This simply means that disciples of Jesus do NOT go through the Wrath of God. Look also at 1 Thessalonians 1:9–10. "For they themselves declare concerning us what manner of entry we had to you, and how you turned to God from idols to serve the living and true God, and to wait for His Son from heaven, whom He raised from the dead, even Jesus who delivers us from the **wrath** [Wrath of God] to come [Jesus delivers us from the Wrath of God to come]." This simply means that Christians do NOT go through the Wrath of God.

Throughout the Bible, **Tribulation** and **Persecution** come from our **Stand** on the **Word of God** and our **Testimony of Jesus**. Notice what John wrote in Revelation 1:9. Again, I will underline a few words.

> I, John, both your brother and companion in the Tribulation and Kingdom and Patience of Jesus Christ, was on the Island that is called Patmos for the Word of God and for the Testimony of Jesus Christ.

Jesus instructs His disciples to "Stand" and to "Overcome" and to be "Faithful unto Death". Therefore, it is important for a disciple of Jesus to understand this Bible Truth:

TRIBULATION and **PERSECUTION**
come from our **STAND**
on the **WORD of GOD** and our **TESTIMONY of JESUS**.

Jesus spoke of these things [Tribulation and Persecution] to His disciples near the close of His ministry in John 16:1–4. Again, I will underline a few words.

> These things I have spoken to you, that you should not be made to stumble. They will put you out of the synagogues; Yes, the time is coming that whoever kills you will think that he offers God service. And these

things they will do to you because they have not known the Father nor Me. <u>But these things I have told you, that when the time comes, you may remember that I told you of them.</u> And these things I did not say to you at the beginning, because I was with you.

Just prior to saying that, Jesus said this in John 15:12–27.

> This is My commandment—that you love one another as I have loved you. Greater love has no one than this, than to lay down one's life for his friends. You are My friends—<u>if you do whatever I command you</u>. No longer do I call you servants, for a servant does not know what his master is doing; but I have called you friends, for all things that I heard from My Father I have made known to you.
>
> You did not choose Me—but I chose you and appointed you that you should go and bear fruit, and that your fruit should remain, that whatever you ask the Father in My name He may give you.
>
> These things I command you—that you love one another. <u>If the world hates you, you know that it hated Me before it hated you.</u> If you were of the world, the world would love its own. Yet because you are not of the world, but I chose you out of the world, therefore the world hates you.
>
> Remember the word that I said to you, "A servant is not greater than his master." <u>If they persecuted Me, they will also persecute you</u> [Tribulation and Persecution]. If they kept My word, they will keep yours also.
>
> <u>But all these things they will do to you</u> for <u>My Name's Sake</u> [Disciples of Jesus will go through Tribulation and Persecution because of their stand on the Word of God and because of their Testimony of Jesus]—because they

do not know Him who sent Me. If I had not come and spoken to them, they would have no sin, but now they have no excuse for their sin.

He who hates Me—hates My Father also. If I had not done among them the works which no one else did, they would have no sin; but now they have seen and also hated both Me and My Father. But this happened that the word might be fulfilled which is written in their law, "They hated Me without a cause."

But when the Helper [the Holy Spirit] comes, whom I shall send to you from the Father, the Spirit of Truth [the Holy Spirit] who proceeds from the Father, He [the Holy Spirit] will testify of Me [Jesus]. And you will also bear witness, because you have been with Me from the beginning.

Jesus instructs His disciples to "Stand" and to "Overcome" and to be "Faithful unto Death". Therefore, it is important for a disciple of Jesus to understand this Bible Truth:

> **TRIBULATION** and **PERSECUTION**
> come from our **STAND**
> on the **WORD of GOD** and our **TESTIMONY of JESUS**.

The Temple was also mentioned in 2 Thessalonians 2:1–5, when Paul taught on the end-time events of the coming Antichrist and the Abomination of Desolation [which occurs inside the Temple].

Now, brethren, concerning the coming of our Lord Jesus Christ and our gathering together to Him, we ask you, not to be soon shaken in mind or troubled, either by spirit or by word or by letter, as if from us, as though the day of Christ had come.

Let no one deceive you by any means; for that Day will not come unless the falling away comes first, and the man of sin [the Antichrist] is revealed, the son of perdition [the Antichrist], who opposes and exalts himself above all that is called God or that is worshipped, so that he [the Antichrist] sits as God in the Temple of God, showing himself that he is God [This event is what the Bible refers to as the "Abomination of Desolation"].

Do you not remember that when I was still with you I told you these things?

As mentioned earlier, many people have been taught that the Rapture occurs prior to the Tribulation and therefore many people have been taught that Christians do not go through the Tribulation. Nevertheless, in the passages of scripture that we saw in Matthew 24:15–22, Mark 13:14–20, Matthew 24:29–31, and Mark 13:24–27, Jesus is clearly teaching His disciples that the "Rapture" occurs after the "Tribulation".

Likewise, many people have been taught that the "Rapture" could occur at any time. Nevertheless, in these same passages of Scripture, the Bible teaches that the "Rapture" will not occur until after the Antichrist commits the event that the Bible refers to as the "Abomination of Desolation" [which occurs inside the Temple].

Therefore, prior to 1948, the biblical sequence of events would be this.

- Israel becomes a nation again.
- The Temple is rebuilt.
- The Abomination of Desolation occurs.
- The Rapture occurs.

Therefore, prior to 1948, if someone was teaching that the "Rapture" could occur at any time, they would be failing to understand that there has to be a Temple, because the event of the "Abomination of Desolation" [which occurs inside the Temple] has to occur before the event of the "Rapture". Likewise, the event of the "Abomination of Desolation" [which occurs inside the Temple] has to occur after the Temple has been rebuilt.

Furthermore, prior to 1948, if someone was teaching that the

"Rapture" could occur at any time, they would be failing to understand that Israel must become a nation again <u>before</u> Israel can rebuild the Temple.

The Temple was also mentioned in a vision that God showed to Daniel.

> And out of one of them came a little horn [the Antichrist] which grew exceedingly great toward the south, toward the east, and toward the Glorious Land [Israel]. And it grew up to the host of heaven; and it cast down some of the host and some of the stars to the ground, and trampled them.
>
> He [the Antichrist] even exalted himself as high as the Prince of the host; and by him [the Antichrist] the daily sacrifices [the Daily Sacrifices at the Temple] were taken away, and the place of His sanctuary was cast down.
>
> Because of his transgression, an army was given over to the horn [the Antichrist] to oppose the daily sacrifices [the Daily Sacrifices at the Temple]; and he [the Antichrist] cast truth down to the ground. He [the Antichrist] did all this and prospered. (Daniel 8:9–12)

There are many other references to the Temple that are part of these end-time events, but because the Temple was destroyed in AD 70, these end-time events have always been hard to understand. Hopefully you can see that prior to Israel becoming a nation (again) in 1948, the biblical sequence of events described in the teachings of Jesus and described in the teachings of Paul, and the sequence of events showed to Daniel in the Book of Daniel, and the sequence of events showed to John in the Book of Revelation were simply hard to understand, because they all mentioned the Temple, and for almost two thousand years prior to 1948, there has been no Temple. Therefore it was tough for folks to simply understand and believe that "What the Bible Said" was actually true.

Please understand:

My Job is NOT to convince you that the Bible is True.

My Job is to Teach you What the Bible Says.

It is the Holy Spirit's Job to convince you that the Bible is True.

Now that Israel is a nation, we can understand the actual biblical sequence of events.

- Israel becomes a nation. This event occurred in 1948.
- Temple is rebuilt—The Bible does not tell us whether the Temple is rebuilt before the Tribulation begins, but it is definitely rebuilt before the Antichrist commits the Abomination of Desolation—Matthew 24:15–-22; Mark 13:14–20; 2 Thessalonians 2:1–5.
- The Abomination of Desolation occurs.
- The Rapture occurs.

In 2 Thessalonians 2:1–5, we are warned about the possibility of being deceived.

> Now, brethren, concerning the coming of our Lord Jesus Christ and our gathering together to Him, we ask you, not to be soon shaken in mind or troubled, either by spirit or by word or by letter, as if from us, as though the day of Christ had come.
>
> <u>Let no one deceive you by any means</u>; for that Day will not come unless the falling away comes first, and the man of sin [the Antichrist] is revealed, the son of perdition [the Antichrist], who opposes and exalts himself above all that is called God or that is worshipped, so that he [the Antichrist] sits as God in the Temple of God, showing himself that he is God [This event is what the Bible refers to as the "Abomination of Desolation"].
>
> Do you not remember that when I was still with you I told you these things?

To understand the Book of Revelation, it is important to understand the actual biblical sequence of events given by Jesus and by Paul and by all other biblical scriptures. The sequence that we read in 2 Thessalonians 2:1–5 is this.

- The Temple is rebuilt.
- The Abomination of Desolation occurs.

Let's compare this sequence with the sequences we saw in other scriptures. In Matthew 24:15–22, it was this.

- The Temple is rebuilt.
- The Abomination of Desolation occurs.
- The Tribulation occurs.
- The Rapture occurs.

In Mark 13:14–20, it was this.

- The Temple is rebuilt.
- The Abomination of Desolation occurs.
- The Tribulation occurs.
- The Rapture occurs.

In Matthew 24:29–31, it was this.

- The Tribulation occurs.
- The sun and moon are darkened.
- The Son of Man comes on the clouds.
- The Rapture occurs.

In Mark 13:24–27, it was this.

- The Tribulation occurs.
- The sun and moon are darkened.
- The Son of Man comes on the clouds.
- The Rapture occurs.

Paul's sequence in 2 Thessalonians 2:1–5 is the same as given by Jesus.

- The Temple is rebuilt.
- The Abomination of Desolation occurs.

If we put together a sequence of what we have so far, it would look like this.

- The Temple is rebuilt—Matthew 24:15–22; Mark 13:14–20; 2 Thessalonians 2:1–5.
- The Abomination of Desolation—Matthew 24:15–22; Mark 13:14–20; 2 Thessalonians 2:1–5.
- The Tribulation—Matthew 24:15–22; Mark 13:14–20; Matthew 24:29–31; Mark 13:24–27.
- Sun and moon are darkened—Matthew 24:29–31; Mark 13:24–27.
- Son of Man coming on the clouds—Matthew 24:29–31; Mark 13:24–27.
- Rapture—Matthew 24:15–22; Mark 13:14–20; Matthew 24:29–31; Mark 13:24–27.

In the above sequences, we see what happens after the Abomination of Desolation [which occurs inside the Temple] toward the end of the Tribulation just before the Rapture. Matthew 24:3–13 offers a picture of what happens at the beginning of the Tribulation. Again, I have underlined a few words to help us "see" the sequence of events:

> Now as He sat on the Mount of Olives, the disciples came to Him privately, saying, "Tell us, when will these things be? And what will be the sign of Your coming, and of the end of the age?"
>
> And Jesus answered and said to them: "Take heed that no one deceives you. For many will come in My name, saying, 'I am the Christ', and will deceive many.
>
> "And you will hear of wars and rumors of wars. See that you are not troubled; for all these things must come to pass, but the end is not yet. For nation will rise against nation, and kingdom against kingdom. And there will be famines, pestilences, and earthquakes in various places.

"All these are the <u>Beginnings of Sorrows</u>.

"<u>Then</u> they will deliver you up to <u>Tribulation</u> and <u>kill you</u>, and you will be hated by all nations <u>for My Name's Sake</u>. And then many will be offended, will betray one another, and will hate one another. Then many false prophets will rise up and deceive many. And because lawlessness will abound, the love of many will grow cold.

"<u>But he who endures to the end</u> shall be saved [Faithful unto Death]."

The sequence here in Matthew 24:3–13 is this.

- Beginnings of Sorrows—this could have begun as early as when Jesus ascended to heaven because there certainly have been wars, rumors of wars, earthquakes, pestilences, and famines since then.
- Tribulation begins and continues—this is the Beginning of the Tribulation.

Putting all these "Sequence of Events" together would look like this.

- Beginnings of sorrows—Matthew 24:3–13.
- Tribulation begins and continues—this is the beginning of the Tribulation—Matthew 24:3–13.
- Temple is rebuilt—The Bible does not tell us whether the Temple is rebuilt before the Tribulation begins, but the Temple is definitely rebuilt before the Antichrist commits the Abomination of Desolation—Matthew 24:15–-22; Mark 13:14–20; 2 Thessalonians 2:1–5.
- Abomination of Desolation—Matthew 24:15–22; Mark 13:14–20; 2 Thessalonians 2:1–5.
- Great Tribulation—In Matthew 24:21–22, Jesus said, "For then there will be <u>Great Tribulation</u>, such as has not been since the beginning of the world until this time, no, nor ever shall be. And unless those days were shortened, no flesh would be saved; but for the elect's sake those days will be shortened."

- In Matthew, Jesus referred to the time toward the end of the Tribulation as the "Great Tribulation". This is the time immediately after the Abomination of Desolation and just before the Rapture—Matthew 24:15–22; Mark 13:14–20; Matthew 24:29–31; Mark 13:24–27.
- Sun and moon are darkened—Matthew 24:29–31; Mark 13:24–27.
- Son of Man coming on the clouds—Matthew 24:29–31, Mark 13:24–27.
- Rapture—Matthew 24:15–22; Mark 13:14–20; Matthew 24:29–31; Mark 13:24–27.

Let's look at other verses that describe the "Rapture".

> Behold, I tell you a mystery: We shall not all sleep, but we shall all be changed—in a moment, in the twinkling of an eye, at the Last Trumpet. For the Trumpet will sound, and the dead in Christ will be raised incorruptible [This event is known as the "Rapture"], and we shall all be changed [This event in known as the "Rapture"]. (1 Corinthians 15:51–52)

In the previous passage of Scripture, Paul wrote that the Rapture occurs at the "Last Trumpet". In 1 Thessalonians 4:15–18, Paul will write that this "Last Trumpet" is actually the "Trumpet of God". Before we read that, let's understand the following:

We will discuss the following in much more detail later in this book and give the actual scripture references, but in the Book of Revelation, we will see Jesus take the Scroll from the hand of God and open it in the following order:

1. The Seven Seals.
2. The First Four Trumpets.
3. The Fifth Trumpet (the First Woe).
4. The Sixth Trumpet (the Second Woe).
   Both the Seven Thunders and the three and a half year [1,260 days] Ministry of the Two Prophets occur during the period of the Sixth Trumpet.

5. The Seventh Trumpet (the Third Woe).
   Some amazing things happen at the Seventh Trumpet, including an Angel Preaching the Gospel to those on the earth prior to the Rapture. The Rapture occurs during the time of the Seventh Trumpet. Then after the Rapture occurs, the Seven Bowls of the Wrath of God are poured out onto an unsaved world.
6. The Seven Bowls of the Wrath of God.

Therefore this "Last Trumpet" is actually the "Seventh Trumpet". In other words, the "Rapture" occurs at the "Seventh Trumpet" prior to the "Wrath of God". Again, I will underline a few words.

> For this we say to you by the Word of the Lord, that we who are alive and remain until the coming of the Lord will by no means precede those who are asleep. For the Lord Himself will descend from heaven with a shout, with the voice of an archangel, and with the <u>Trumpet of God</u>. And the dead in Christ will rise first [This event is known as the "Rapture"].
>
> Then we who are alive and remain shall be caught up together with them in the clouds to meet the Lord in the air [This event is known as the "Rapture"].
>
> And thus we shall always be with the Lord. Therefore comfort one another with these words. (1 Thessalonians 4:15–18)

The sequence here is that Jesus descends from heaven with a shout, with the voice of an archangel, and with the Trumpet of God, and then the Rapture occurs.

Here is the way the Rapture and the Wrath of God (which follows the Rapture) is described in the Book of Revelation.

> Then I looked, and behold, a white cloud, and on the cloud sat One like the Son of Man, having on His head a golden crown, and in His hand a sharp sickle. And

another angel came out of the Temple [this is the Temple in Heaven], crying with a loud voice to Him who sat on the cloud, "Thrust in Your sickle and reap, for the time has come for You to reap, for the harvest of the earth is ripe." [What follows is a "picture" of the Rapture.]

So He who sat on the cloud thrust in His sickle on the earth, and the earth was reaped [Rapture].

Then another angel came out of the Temple which is in Heaven, he also having a sharp sickle. And another angel came out from the altar, who had power over fire, and he cried out with a loud cry to him who had the sharp sickle, saying, "Thrust in your sharp sickle and gather the clusters of the vine of the earth, for her grapes are fully ripe." [What follows is a "picture" of the Wrath of God.]

So the angel thrust his sickle into the earth and gathered the vine of the earth, and threw it into the great winepress of the Wrath of God [Wrath of God]. And the winepress was trampled outside the city, and blood came out of the winepress, up to the horses' bridles, for one thousand six hundred furlongs [160-plus miles]. (Revelation 14:14–20)

The sequence here is the Son of Man on a cloud, then the Rapture, and then the Wrath of God.

The sequence of these last three passages of scripture can be seen as follows.

- Last Trumpet—1 Corinthians 15:51–52.
- Jesus descends from heaven with a shout, with the voice of an archangel, and with the Trumpet of God—1 Thessalonians 4:15–18.
- Son of Man on a Cloud—Revelation 14:14–20.
- Rapture—1 Corinthians 15:51–52; 1 Thessalonians 4:15–18; Revelation 14:14–20.
- Wrath of God—Revelation 14:14–20.

Putting the entire sequence together, we get a clear picture of "What Does the Bible Say?" This is the actual biblical "Sequence of Events" that we have seen so far.

- Beginnings of Sorrows—This could have begun as early as when Jesus ascended to heaven because there have been wars, rumors of wars, etc. since that time—Matthew 24:3–13.
- Tribulation begins and continues—Matthew 24:3–13.
- Temple is rebuilt—the Bible does not tell us whether the Temple is rebuilt before the Tribulation begins, but the Temple is definitely rebuilt before the Antichrist commits the Abomination of Desolation—Matthew 24:15–22; Mark 13:14–20; 2 Thessalonians 2:1–5.
- Abomination of Desolation—Matthew 24:15–22; Mark 13:14–20; 2 Thessalonians 2:1–5.
- Great Tribulation—In Matthew 24:21–22, Jesus said, "For then there will be Great Tribulation, such as has not been since the beginning of the world until this time, no, nor ever shall be. And unless those days were shortened, no flesh would be saved; but for the elect's sake those days will be shortened."
- In Matthew, Jesus referred to the time toward the end of the Tribulation as the "Great Tribulation". This is the time immediately after the Abomination of Desolation and just before the Rapture—Matthew 24:15–22; Mark 13:14–20; Matthew 24:29–31; Mark 13:24–27.
- Sun and moon are darkened—Matthew 24:29–31; Mark 13:24–27.
- Last Trumpet—1 Corinthians 15:51–52.
- Jesus descends from heaven with a shout, with the voice of an archangel, and with the Trumpet of God—1 Thessalonians 4:15–18.
- Son of Man coming on the clouds—Matthew 24:29–31; Mark 13:24–27; Revelation 14:14–20.
- Rapture—Matthew 24:15–22; Mark 13:14–20; Matthew 24:29–31; Mark 13:24–27; 1 Corinthians 15:51–52; 1 Thessalonians 4:15–18; Revelation 14:14–20.
- Wrath of God—Revelation 14:14–20.

Jesus instructs His disciples to "Stand" and to "Overcome" and to be "Faithful unto Death". Therefore, it is important for a disciple of Jesus to understand this Bible Truth:

> **TRIBULATION** and **PERSECUTION**
> come from our **STAND**
> on the **WORD of GOD** and our **TESTIMONY of JESUS**.

As we read the first three verses of the Book of Revelation, it is easy to see that God definitely wants us to understand the actual biblical sequence of these end-time events. God shows everything to Jesus, who sends His angel to show everything to His servant John, who writes a book, so that we—even two thousand years later—can read and understand the actual biblical sequence of these end-time events. God wants us to understand!

> The Revelation of Jesus Christ, which God gave Him [Jesus] to show His servants—things which must shortly take place. And He [Jesus] sent and signified it by His angel to His servant John, who bore witness to the Word of God, and to the Testimony of Jesus Christ, to all things that he saw.
>
> Blessed is he who reads and those who hear the words of this prophecy, and keep those things which are written in it; for the time is near. (Revelation 1:1–3)

CHAPTER 2

Jesus Wants Us to Understand

When the disciples of Jesus asked Him to tell them about the end-time events, Jesus began by saying, "Take heed that no one deceives you" (Matthew 24:4).

Jesus was not giving this warning to the nation of Israel (as some have been encouraged to believe), but Jesus was giving this warning to His disciples.

If your name is written in the Lamb's Book of Life, then Jesus sees you as a "disciple". You may not currently see yourself as a "disciple", but if you are born again, then Jesus sees you as a "disciple". Furthermore, if you are a disciple of Jesus, then you are commanded to obey the commandments of Jesus and to be "Faithful unto Death". Therefore, when a disciple of Jesus comes under Persecution and Tribulation, it will be because of their Stand on the Word of God and because of their Testimony of Jesus.

With that Bible truth in mind, let's take another look at Matthew 24:3–13. I will underline a few words.

> Now as He sat on the Mount of Olives, the disciples came to Him privately, saying, "Tell us, when will these things be? And what will be the sign of Your coming, and of the end of the age?"
>
> And Jesus answered and said to them: "Take heed that no one <u>deceives</u> you. For many will come in My name, saying, 'I am the Christ,' and will <u>deceive many</u>. And you will hear of wars and rumors of wars. See that you are

not troubled; for all these things must come to pass, but the end is not yet.

"For nation will rise against nation, and kingdom against kingdom. And there will be famines, pestilences, and earthquakes in various places.

"All these are the <u>Beginnings of Sorrows</u>. [This could have begun as early as when Jesus ascended to heaven—because there certainly have been wars and rumors of wars and earthquakes and pestilences and famines since that time.]

"<u>Then</u> they will deliver you up to <u>Tribulation</u> and <u>kill you</u>, and you will be <u>hated by all nations</u> for <u>My Name's sake</u> [because of the Name of Jesus].

"And then many will be offended, will betray one another, and will hate one another. <u>Then many false prophets will rise up</u> and <u>deceive many</u>. And because lawlessness will abound, the love of many will grow cold.

"But <u>he who endures to the end</u> shall be saved. [<u>Faithful unto Death</u>]"

Jesus instructs His disciples to "Stand" and to "Overcome" and to be "Faithful unto Death". Therefore, it is important for a disciple of Jesus to understand this Bible Truth:

> **TRIBULATION** and **PERSECUTION**
> come from our **STAND**
> on the **WORD of GOD** and our **TESTIMONY of JESUS**.

When Mark records this same event, Mark gives us the additional information that the disciples who had come to Jesus in private were actually Peter, James, John, and Andrew. When these four disciples asked Jesus about these end-time events, Mark records that the first words that Jesus spoke to them—in answer to their question—was a clear warning: "Take heed that no one deceives you" (Mark 13:5).

Jesus was not giving this warning to the nation of Israel (as some have been encouraged to believe), but Jesus was giving this warning to His disciples. Picture yourself as being there, listening to Jesus, as He answered the question concerning these end-time events for Peter, James, John, and Andrew. Again, I will underline a few words.

> Now as He sat on the Mount of Olives opposite the Temple—Peter, James, John, and Andrew asked Him privately, "Tells us, when will these things be? And what will be the sign when all these things will be fulfilled?"
>
> And Jesus answering them, began to say, "Take heed that no one <u>deceives</u> you. For many will come in My name, saying, 'I am He,' and will <u>deceive many</u>.
>
> "But when you hear of wars and rumors of wars, do not be troubled; for such things must happen, but the end is not yet. For nation will rise against nation, and kingdom against kingdom. And there will be earthquakes in various places, and there will be famines and troubles.
>
> "These are the <u>Beginnings of Sorrows</u>. [This could have begun as early as when Jesus ascended to heaven—because there certainly have been wars and rumors of wars and earthquakes and pestilences and famines since that time.]
>
> "But watch out for yourselves, for they will deliver you up to the councils, and you will be beaten in the synagogues. You will be brought before rulers and kings <u>for My sake</u> [because of the <u>Name of Jesus</u>], for a Testimony to them.
>
> "And the gospel must first be preached to all the nations.

"But <u>when they arrest you and deliver you up</u>, do not worry beforehand, or premeditate what you will speak. But whatever is given you in that hour, speak that; <u>for it is not you who speak—but the Holy Spirit</u>.

"Now brother will betray brother to death, and a father his child; and children will rise up against parents and cause them to be <u>put to death</u>. And <u>you will be hated</u> by all <u>for My Name's sake</u> [because of the Name of Jesus].

"But <u>he who endures to the end</u> will be saved [<u>Faithful unto Death</u>]." (Mark 13:3–13)

Jesus instructs His disciples to "Stand" and to "Overcome" and to be "Faithful unto Death". Therefore, it is important for a disciple of Jesus to understand this Bible Truth:

> **TRIBULATION** and **PERSECUTION**
> come from our **STAND**
> on the **WORD of GOD** and our **TESTIMONY of JESUS**.

When Jesus first spoke of the "Abomination of Desolation" [which occurs inside the Temple], Matthew and Mark emphasized the importance of that end-time event by adding, "Whoever reads, let him understand" (Matthew 24:15) and "Let the reader understand" (Mark 13:14). In both accounts, Jesus referred to this event as the "Abomination of Desolation" spoken of by Daniel the prophet. Therefore, let's look at the book of Daniel and see if the Temple is mentioned in any of Daniel's end-time prophetic visions. The first place we should look is Daniel 9:20–27. I will underline a few words.

> Now while I was speaking, praying, and confessing my sin and the sin of <u>my people Israel</u> and presenting my supplication before the LORD my God for the Holy Mountain of my God—yes—while I was speaking in

prayer, the man <u>Gabriel</u>, whom I had seen in the vision at the beginning, being caused to fly swiftly, reached me about the time of the evening offering.

And he informed me, and talked with me, and said, "O Daniel, I have now come forth to give you skill to <u>understand</u>. At the beginning of your supplications the command went out, and I have come to tell you, for you are greatly beloved; therefore consider the matter, and <u>understand</u> the vision:

"Seventy weeks [70 sevens or 70 seven-year periods or 490 years] are determined for your people [Israel] and for your holy city [Jerusalem], to finish the transgression, to make an end of sins, to make reconciliation for iniquity, to bring in everlasting righteousness, to seal up vision and prophecy, and to anoint the Most Holy.

"Know therefore and <u>understand</u>, that from the going forth of the command to restore and build Jerusalem until Messiah the Prince [Jesus], there shall be seven weeks and sixty-two weeks [This is a total of 69 weeks or 69 sevens or 69 seven-year periods or 483 years]; the street shall be built again, and the wall, even in troublesome times.

"And after the sixty-two weeks [483 years] Messiah shall be cut off, but not for Himself; and the people of the prince who is to come shall destroy the city [Jerusalem] and the sanctuary [the Temple]. The end of it shall be with a flood, and till the end of the war desolations are determined.

"Then he shall confirm a covenant with many for one week [one seven or one seven-year period or 7 years]; but in the middle of the week [in the middle of this seven-year covenant with many] he [the Antichrist] shall bring an end to sacrifice and offering [after three and a half years, the Antichrist will break the covenant and <u>Stop the Daily Sacrifices at the Temple</u>]. And on the wing of abominations shall be one who makes desolate, even until the consummation, which is determined, is poured out on the desolate."

This is an amazing passage of Scripture and it is very important for our understanding of the Book of Revelation because this prophecy shows that God has determined a certain period of time—seventy sevens—seventy seven-year periods—490 years—in which God will complete ALL of His promises to Israel. This 490-year period is actually a 483-year period—that has a definite beginning and a definite end—plus one final seven-year period. The 483-year period begins with "the going forth of the command to restore and build Jerusalem" and ends with "Messiah the Prince" (Daniel 9:20–27). We will see later that the final seven-year period is actually what we call the "Seven-year Tribulation" described by John in the Book of Revelation.

Before we go any further, let's understand who Daniel was, and where Daniel was, and why he was there. Giving a complete background of all the events leading up to Daniel and why God had caused the nation of Israel to go into captivity in Babylon for seventy years is not within the scope of this book, but here is a quick summary.

- God created the earth and placed Adam and Eve in the Garden of Eden.
- The serpent [Satan] used deception to get Adam to turn over the authority of the earth which God had given him, and Satan gained control over the earth. Sin, death, and disease entered the earth. God removed Adam and Eve from the Garden of Eden to prevent them from eating of the Tree of Life and living forever in that fallen state.
- Years later, humanity was so corrupt and sinful that God handpicked Noah and his family and basically started over by causing the Flood, which wiped out everyone else.
- After the Flood, some of Noah's descendants began to build the tower of Babel, and God confused their languages to stop that

- building project, which was in direct disobedience to the Word of God, and God scattered the people.
- This town later became Babylon (mentioned in Revelation), and Abram was born near that area in Ur of the Chaldeans.
- God handpicked Abram and said this to him in Genesis 12:1–3.

> Now the LORD had said to Abram, "Get out of your country, from your family and from your father's house, to a land that I will show you. I will make you a great nation [Israel]; I will Bless you and make your name great; and you shall be a Blessing. I will Bless those who Bless you, and I will curse him who curses you; and in you all the families of the earth shall be Blessed."

- God continued to make promises to Abram, changed his name to Abraham, and gave him a son, Isaac.
- God gave Isaac a son, Jacob, and God later changed his name to Israel.
- Jacob (Israel) had twelve sons—who became the twelve tribes of Israel mentioned in Revelation.
- For the first 2,000 years after Adam, God dealt with humanity according to grace.
- After God used Moses to bring the children of Israel out of their bondage in Egypt, God gave the Law through Moses and dealt with Israel according to the Law for the next 2,000 years.
- When Israel broke the Law, there were consequences; one came because the nation of Israel was not obeying the Sabbath rest instructions. The result was Babylon conquered Israel, destroyed the Temple (which David's son Solomon had built), and took Israel into captivity.
- Granted there were people and kings who were committed to God, but basically, God's experience with Israel was one of "Persistent Unfaithfulness".
- God's punishment for Israel was the captivity in Babylon for seventy years, and that is where we find Daniel praying that God would return Israel to the land God had given them and cause the Temple and the city of Jerusalem to be rebuilt.

- God showed Daniel in Daniel 9:20–27 that the Temple and Jerusalem would be rebuilt and showed him when the promised Messiah (Jesus) would come.
- God showed Daniel that the second Temple would be destroyed after the Messiah was "cut off" (after Jesus accomplished what He was sent to the earth to accomplish during His first coming).
- God showed Daniel that the seventy sevens were actually sixty-nine sevens plus one final seven. We will understand later that this final seven is the final seven years John later wrote about in the Book of Revelation.
- God showed Daniel that the Antichrist would come and stop the daily sacrifices [the Daily Sacrifices at the Temple] in the middle of a seven-year covenant with many—during these final seven years. By doing so, God was also showing Daniel that a third Temple would definitely be built.
- The Book of Revelation is all about God keeping His promises to Israel, and to do that, the Temple must be rebuilt. God will keep His Word to save Israel not because of anything Israel has done but because God always keeps His Word.
- The Book of Revelation will show us that once God has kept ALL of His promises to Israel, He will then cause the earth to have a period of Sabbath rest with Jesus ruling and reigning from Jerusalem for 1,000 years while Satan is locked up in a bottomless pit so that Satan cannot deceive the nations during that time.
- Then after the judgment, there will be a New Heaven and a New Earth.

Ezekiel was another prophet who was in captivity in Babylon during the same time as Daniel. Listen as God speaks to Ezekiel in this amazing prophecy. I will underline a few words.

> You also, son of man, take a clay tablet and lay it before you, and portray on it a city, Jerusalem. Lay siege against it, build a siege wall against it, and heap up a mound against it; set camps against it also, and place battering rams against it all around. Moreover take for yourself an iron plate, and set it as an iron wall between you and the

city. Set your face against it, and it shall be besieged, and you shall lay siege against it. <u>This will be a sign to the house of Israel.</u>

Lie also on your left side, and lay <u>the iniquity of the house of Israel</u> upon it. According to the number of the days that you lie on it, you shall bear their iniquity.

For <u>I have laid on you the years of their iniquity</u>, according to the number of the days, three hundred and ninety days [390 days]; so you shall bear <u>the iniquity of the house of Israel</u>.

And when you have completed them, lie again on your right side; then you shall bear <u>the iniquity of the house of Judah</u> forty days [40 days]. <u>I have laid on you a day for each year.</u> (Ezekiel 4:1–6)

This passage clearly shows that one day equals one year. Therefore 390 days equals 390 years of punishment for the iniquity of the house of Israel and 40 days equals 40 years of punishment for the iniquity of the house of Judah. Adding all of this together equals a total of 430 years of punishment for the iniquity of the nation of Israel.

The first decree to release Israel from their captivity in Babylon was by the Persian King Cyrus—exactly seventy years to the day—from when Israel went into captivity. According to this prophecy that God gave to Ezekiel, there are a total of 430 years of punishment for the iniquity of the nation of Israel. We subtract the 70 years of Israel's captivity in Babylon and that leaves a remaining 360 years of punishment for the iniquity of the nation of Israel.

During this initial 70 years of captivity, Israel was under the rule of the Babylonians. Even after Israel returned to Jerusalem and rebuilt the Temple, its people were still under Persian rule. Then Israel was conquered by the Greeks and later by the Romans even until the time of Jesus. When the Romans destroyed the Temple and Jerusalem in AD 70, the Israelites were scattered throughout the world and the nation of Israel ceased to exist as a nation for almost 2,000 years.

So what of the remaining 360 years of punishment for the iniquity of the nation of Israel?

Look at what the Lord said to Moses on Mount Sinai—when Israel first came out of Egypt—instructing him to speak these words to the children of Israel: "And after all this, if you do not obey Me, then <u>I will punish you seven times more for your sins</u>" (Leviticus 26:18).

This is repeated three more times for emphasis.

> Then, if you walk contrary to Me, and are not willing to obey Me, <u>I will bring on you seven times more plagues, according to your sins.</u> (Leviticus 26:21)

> And if by these things you are not reformed by Me, but walk contrary to Me, then I also will walk contrary to you, and <u>I will punish you yet seven times for your sins.</u> (Leviticus 26:23–24)

> And after all this, if you do not obey Me, but walk contrary to Me, then I also will walk contrary to you in fury; and <u>I, even I, will chastise you seven times</u> for your sins. (Leviticus 26:27–28)

The remaining 360 years of punishment for the iniquity of the nation of Israel—times seven—equals 2,520 years of punishment.

God had given Israel a very sophisticated calendar being both lunar and solar. The people of Israel have a calendar that uses a 360-day lunar (and prophetic) year and adds leap months on occasion so it matches with the solar calendar.

If we convert the 2,520 years of punishment in this prophecy into the actual number of days, we can convert the actual number of days back into our solar years by dividing by 365.25 days per year, which would also adjust for our leap years: 2,520 years of punishment times 360 days per year equals 907,200 days of punishment for the iniquity of Israel. That divided by 365.25 days per year equals 2,483.778 years of punishment for the iniquity of Israel.

I hate to bore you with the math, but the decree of Cyrus went forth in 536 BC. Let's treat that year as a negative number: negative 536 plus a positive 2,483 equals 1,947; we add 1 to that (since there is no AD 0) and get 1,948.

Israel became a nation (again) in 1948. This ended the 2,520 years of punishment for the nation of Israel. In 1948, Israel once again became a nation after enduring over 2,500 years of God's punishment for the "Persistent Unfaithfulness of Israel"!

For almost 2,000 years prior to when Israel became a nation (again) in 1948, it was very hard for folks to understand the Book of Revelation—because so many of the prophecies related to the Temple—but the nation of Israel and the Temple had both been destroyed in AD 70. There were prophecies about "Measuring the Temple"; there were prophecies about the Antichrist stopping the "Daily Sacrifices" at the Temple; and there were prophecies about the "Abomination of Desolation" which the Antichrist would commit in the most Holy Place inside the Temple—the Holy of Holies.

When Israel became a nation (again) in 1948, I am sure that many people realized that this was a fulfillment of Bible prophecy. Nevertheless, I wonder how many people actually understood and realized how precisely God had fulfilled that prophecy—beginning with what the Lord spoke to Moses on Mount Sinai—when Israel had just come out of Egypt—prior to spending 40 years in the wilderness and prior to entering the Promised Land. God's prophecies are amazing and God always keeps His WORD.

Israel is the only nation in the history of the world that has ever returned as a nation, once they have been destroyed as a nation. Therefore, it is very important for us to understand that God takes his prophecies seriously—and the prophecies in the Bible describing the end-time events to come are very serious indeed.

Please understand:

My Job is NOT to convince you that the Bible is True.

My Job is to Teach you What the Bible Says.

It is the Holy Spirit's Job to convince you that the Bible is True.

With that in mind, let's take a quick look at a passage of scripture written over a hundred years before Cyrus was born. In other words, years before this person was even born, God knew he would become King of Persia and God called him by name, "Cyrus". This would be that Cyrus King of Persia who would rule over the Babylonian empire and who in 536 BC would issue the decree to rebuild the Temple and who would return over 50,000 of the children of Israel to their homeland thus ending their captivity in Babylon.

Look at what God says in Isaiah 44:28.

> Who says of Cyrus, "He is My shepherd, and he shall perform all My pleasure, saying to Jerusalem, 'You shall be built' and to the Temple, 'Your foundation shall be laid.'"

God's prophecies are amazing and God always keeps His WORD. Look at what God says in Isaiah 46:9–13.

> Remember the former things of old, for I am God, and there is no other: I am God, and there is none like Me, declaring the end from the beginning, and from ancient times things that are not yet done, saying, "My counsel shall stand, and I will do all My pleasure," calling a bird of prey from the east, the man who executes My council, from a far country.
>
> Indeed I have spoken it; I will also bring it to pass.
>
> I have purposed it; I will also do it.
>
> Listen to Me you stubborn-hearted, who are far from righteousness: I bring My Righteousness near, it shall not be far off; My Salvation shall not linger. And I will place Salvation in Zion, for Israel My glory.

God's prophecies are amazing and God always keeps His WORD. In the Book of Revelation, we see prophecies that declare that during the seven years of Tribulation, the world will endure what God calls His "Four Severe Judgments"—the sword, famine, wild beasts, and pestilence. In Revelation, John is shown that one half of the population of the earth is killed by one of these "Four Severe Judgments". During the first half of what we call the "Seven-year Tribulation", John is shown that one fourth of the earth is killed. During the second half of the "Seven-year Tribulation", John is shown that another one third of the earth is killed. Therefore a total of one half of the total population of the earth is killed.

Scripture tells us that this is God's judgment on the "Persistent Unfaithfulness of the World". For seven years, God will cause the people of the world to endure Tribulation and Persecution—seven years of His "Four Severe Judgments"—seven years of the sword, famine, wild beasts, and pestilence—all because of the "Persistent Unfaithfulness of the World".

Before you deem this judgment too harsh, please understand that God has already caused the nation of Israel to endure over 2,500 years of Tribulation and Persecution—over 2,500 years of His "Four Severe Judgments"—over 2,500 years of the sword, famine, wild beasts, and pestilence—all because of the "Persistent Unfaithfulness of Israel".

But God still has promises to keep to Israel.

Therefore, during the first three and a half years of the "Seven-year Tribulation", God will "handpick" and "set apart" and "seal" 144,000—12,000 each from the twelve tribes of Israel. These are "selected" and "set apart" and "sealed"—but they are not yet "Saved"—they are not yet "Disciples of Jesus". God will use the Fifth Trumpet (the five-month torment on all but the 144,000) to make a distinction between the 144,000 and all others. Revelation 9:5 states, "In those days, men will seek death and will not find it; they will desire to die, and death will flee from them." All of this will happen during the first three and a half years of the "Seven-year Tribulation".

Then during the second three and a half years of the "Seven-year Tribulation", God will send the two witnesses—His Two Prophets discussed in Revelation 11:1–14—and they will actually teach "Jesus is the Messiah" to the 144,000—from the Temple in Jerusalem—for three and a half years.

During their 1,260-day (three and a half year) ministry, every single one of the 144,000 will be saved—12,000 each from the twelve tribes of Israel will be saved—and every single one will become a disciple of Jesus. In fact, every single one of these 144,000 will be "Faithful unto Death" and we will see them in heaven—<u>prior to the Rapture</u>—and they are described as "ones who follow the Lamb wherever He goes" (Revelation 14:1–5).

All of this will happen during the second three and a half years of the "Seven-year Tribulation". Therefore, Israel will be saved—and God's promise to save Israel will be fulfilled—and all of this will occur prior to the Rapture.

Since Christians are in the world, Christians will endure what the world endures during those final seven years—during the "Seven-year Tribulation". During those seven years of God's "Four Severe Judgments", the world (and the Christians in the world) will endure seven years of the sword, famine, wild beasts, and pestilence—all because of the "Persistent Unfaithfulness of the World".

Those seven years will be tough, but those who are disciples of Jesus—those who have their names written in the Lamb's Book of Life—those who obey the commandments of Jesus—will have the opportunity to take a Stand for the <u>Word of God</u> and for their <u>Testimony of Jesus</u> and will be given the opportunity to be "<u>Faithful unto Death</u>".

In Revelation 1–3, Jesus uses the Letters to the Angels of the Seven Churches to instruct His disciples to "Overcome" and to be "Faithful unto Death." Jesus ends His message to His disciples in each of the seven churches with two identical statements.

1. Jesus makes certain promises "To him who Overcomes" [<u>Faithful unto Death</u>].
2. Jesus encourages His disciples to <u>Understand</u> and He continues to repeat the phrase "He who has an ear, let him hear what the Spirit says to the churches."

In Revelation 12:11—the Bible gives instructions on exactly how to "Overcome": "And they overcame him [Satan] by the <u>Blood of the Lamb</u> and by the <u>Word of their Testimony</u>, and <u>they did not love their lives to the death</u> [Faithful unto Death]."

Ask the Lord to help you understand what He is saying to His disciples in the following four passages about being "<u>Faithful unto Death</u>".

> For whoever desires to save his life will lose it, but whoever loses his life for My sake will find it [<u>Faithful unto Death</u>]. (Matthew 16:25)

For whoever desires to save his life will lose it, but whoever loses his life for My sake and the gospel's will save it [Faithful unto Death]. (Mark 8:35)

For whoever desires to save his life will lose it, but whoever loses his life for My sake will save it [Faithful unto Death]. (Luke 9:24)

He who loves his life will lose it, and he who hates his life in this world will keep it for eternal life [Faithful unto Death]. (John 12:25)

Jesus instructs His disciples to "Stand" and to "Overcome" and to be "Faithful unto Death". Therefore, it is important for a disciple of Jesus to understand this Bible Truth:

> **TRIBULATION** and **PERSECUTION**
> come from our **STAND**
> on the **WORD of GOD** and our **TESTIMONY of JESUS**.

Let's return to Daniel's seventy-week vision and apply the same mathematical analysis we used in Ezekiel's prophecy.

There were actually four decrees to rebuild Jerusalem; the first was the decree of King Cyrus in 536 BC which is spoken of at the end of 2 Chronicles and also at the beginning of the book of Ezra. The fourth was the one spoken of in the book of Nehemiah—the decree of King Artaxerxes in 445 BC—whereby the wall of the city was actually rebuilt, the subject of the book of Nehemiah.

Sir Robert Anderson published *The Coming Prince* in 1895; the book is still in print. His best estimate of the date of the decree of King Artaxerxes was March 14, 445 BC.

Daniel is told that there will be seventy sevens—seventy seven-year periods—a period of seventy times seven years—490 years—for God to complete ALL of His promises to Israel. Daniel is told that there will be seven sevens and sixty-two sevens [a total of sixty-nine seven-year periods or 483 years] from the time of the command to restore and build Jerusalem until Messiah the Prince [Jesus]. Daniel is also told there will also be one more seven, the final seven years. The 483 years plus the final seven years equals 490 years, seventy seven-year periods (seventy sevens).

As mentioned earlier, God had given Israel a very sophisticated calendar being both lunar and solar. The people of Israel have a calendar that uses a 360-day lunar (and prophetic) year and adds leap months on occasion so it matches with the solar calendar.

If we convert the 483 years into the actual number of days, we can convert the actual number of days back into our solar years by dividing by 365.25 days per year, which would also adjust for our leap years: 483 years times 360 days per year equals 173,880 days. That divided by 365.25 days per year equals 476.057 years.

The decree of King Artaxerxes was 445 BC. Let's treat that year as a negative number: negative 445 plus a positive 476 equals 31; we add 1 to that (since there is no AD 0) and get 32. In his book *The Coming Prince*, Anderson figured the exact day—April 6, AD 32, his best approximation of the date when Jesus entered Jerusalem before the Passover when He was crucified. This was the first 483 years of Daniel's seventy sevens (490 year) vision.

Again, I hate to bore you with the math, but it was 483 years from the "command to restore and build Jerusalem" until the "Messiah the Prince"—from 445 BC until 32 AD—and the total (seventy sevens) prophecy of 490 years minus these 483 years leaves seven years remaining.

We looked at Daniel 9:20–27, in which God told Daniel there were seventy sevens (490 years) determined for Israel and Jerusalem to accomplish six things.

- to finish the transgression
- to make an end of sins
- to make reconciliation for iniquity
- to bring in everlasting righteousness
- to seal up vision and prophecy
- to anoint the Most Holy

You could make the case that Jesus accomplished some but not all of the six things on the list. So some—but not all—were accomplished in that initial 483-year period.

Remember when Jesus was on the cross and said, "It is finished!"? (John 19:30).

It is as if God somehow hit a stopwatch—reserving those final seven years—reserving that final seven-year period—reserving the seven-year period that we call the "Seven-year Tribulation"—reserving the final seven years that God will use to complete ALL of His promises to Israel.

In other words, for almost 2,000 years, God has been reserving those final seven years!

Here is wisdom: when God takes the Scroll in His right hand (Revelation 5:1), God is then ready to start those final seven years. God is then ready to fulfill ALL of His promises to Israel!

Then, in Revelation 6:1, when Jesus opens the First Seal,

- That will start the final seven years of Daniel's seventy sevens vision.
- That will start the beginning of the "Seven-year Tribulation".
- That will start the final seven years during which God will keep ALL of His promises to Israel.
- And according to what we saw in Daniel 9:20–27, that will also start a period of three and a half years for Israel—the first half of a seven-year covenant with many—which may give the nation of Israel an opportunity to rebuild the Temple (if the Temple has not already been rebuilt by that time).
- Once the Temple is rebuilt, Israel will start the Daily Sacrifices at the Temple in Jerusalem.
- Then three and a half years after the "Seven-year Tribulation" begins—halfway through a seven-year covenant with many, the prince who is to come—the Antichrist—will enter Jerusalem with an army and <u>Stop the Daily Sacrifices</u>.

Putting the entire sequence together, we get a clear picture of "What Does the Bible Say?" This is the actual biblical "<u>Sequence of Events</u>" that we have seen so far.

- Jesus, the Messiah, accomplishes what He was sent to the earth to accomplish during His first coming: "For God so loved the

world that He gave His only begotten Son, that whoever believes in Him should not perish but have everlasting life" (John 3:16).
- You and I now have the opportunity to become disciples of Jesus.

> But what does it [the Scripture] say? "The WORD is near you, in your Mouth and in your Heart"—that is the Word of Faith which we preach—that if you confess with your mouth the Lord Jesus and believe in your heart that God has raised Him from the dead—you will be Saved. For with the heart one believes unto Righteousness, and with the mouth confession is made unto Salvation. (Romans 10:8–10)

- Jesus commands His disciples to be "Faithful unto Death"—Matthew 16:25; Mark 8:35; Luke 9:24; John 12:25.
- Beginnings of Sorrows—This could have begun as early as when Jesus ascended to heaven because there certainly have been wars, rumors of wars, earthquakes, etc. since that time—Matthew 24:3–13; Mark 13:3–13.
- The disciples of Jesus began to be persecuted and were "Faithful unto Death".

> And they stoned Stephen as he was calling on God and saying, "Lord Jesus, receive my spirit." Then he knelt down and cried out with a loud voice, "Lord, do not charge them with this sin." And when he had said this, he fell asleep. Now Saul [who later became the great "Apostle Paul"] was consenting to his death. At that time a great persecution arose against the church which was at Jerusalem; and they were all scattered throughout the regions of Judea and Samaria, except the apostles. And devout men carried Stephen to his burial, and made great lamentation over him. As for Saul, he made havoc of the church, entering every house, and dragging off men and women, committing them to prison. Therefore those who were scattered went everywhere preaching the WORD. (Acts 7:59–8:4)

- The Temple and Jerusalem are destroyed in AD 70 by the Roman Empire; over one million are killed, and the children of Israel are scattered throughout the earth in exile and without a homeland. Israel ceases to exist as a nation for almost 2,000 years.
- The children of Israel continue to endure God's "Four Severe Judgments"—the sword, famine, wild beasts, and pestilence. Israel endures over 2,500 years of God's punishment for the iniquity of the nation of Israel beginning with its seventy-year captivity in Babylon during the time of Daniel and continuing through the years of the World War II Holocaust—which ended in 1945. Israel endures over 2,500 years of God's punishment for the "Persistent Unfaithfulness of Israel"—Ezekiel 4:1–6; Leviticus 26:18–28.
- Israel becomes a nation (again) in 1948; that ends the over 2,500 years of God's punishment for the "Persistent Unfaithfulness of Israel". God honors His promise and returns Israel to its homeland in 1948.

At some point in the future,

- God takes the Scroll in His right hand; He is ready to start the final seven years and fulfill ALL of His promises to Israel—Revelation 5:1; Daniel 9:20–27.
- There is a seven-year covenant with many—which may give the nation of Israel an opportunity to rebuild the Temple (if the Temple has not already been rebuilt by that time)—Daniel 9:20–27.
- Jesus opens the First Seal to start the "Seven year Tribulation"—Revelation 6:1.
- Tribulation begins and continues—Matthew 24:3–13.
- The "Seven-year Tribulation" is God's punishment for the "Persistent Unfaithfulness of the World". This is seven years of what God calls His "Four Severe Judgments"—the sword, famine, wild beasts, and pestilence. Since Christians are in the world, Christians will experience what the world experiences and Christians will endure what the world endures—during the Tribulation.

- God will use these final seven years to fulfill ALL of His promises to Israel—Daniel 9:20–27.
- Temple is rebuilt—the Bible does not tell us whether the Temple is rebuilt before the Tribulation begins, but the Temple is definitely rebuilt before the Antichrist commits the Abomination of Desolation—Matthew 24:15–22; Mark 13:14–20; 2 Thessalonians 2:1–5.
- Israel starts the Daily Sacrifices—Daniel 9:20–27.
- The Antichrist enters Jerusalem with an army and <u>Stops the Daily Sacrifices</u> at the Temple—Daniel 9:20–27.
- Abomination of Desolation—Matthew 24:15–22; Mark 13:14–20; 2 Thessalonians 2:1–5.
- Great Tribulation—In Matthew 24:21–22, Jesus said, "For then there will be <u>Great Tribulation</u>, such as has not been since the beginning of the world until this time, no, nor ever shall be. And unless those days were shortened, no flesh would be saved; but for the elect's sake those days will be shortened."
- In Matthew, Jesus referred to the time toward the end of the Tribulation as the "Great Tribulation". This is the time immediately after the Abomination of Desolation and just before the Rapture—Matthew 24:15–22; Mark 13:14–20; Matthew 24:29–31; Mark 13:24–27.
- Sun and moon are darkened—Matthew 24:29–31; Mark 13:24–27.
- Last Trumpet—1 Corinthians 15:51–52.
- Jesus descends from heaven with a shout, with the voice of an archangel, and with the Trumpet of God—1 Thessalonians 4:15–18.
- Son of Man coming on the clouds—Matthew 24:29–31; Mark 13:24–27; Revelation 14:14–20.
- Rapture—Matthew 24:15–22; Mark 13:14–20; Matthew 24:29–31; Mark 13:24–27; 1 Corinthians 15:51–52; 1 Thessalonians 4:15–18; Revelation 14:14–20.
- Wrath of God—Revelation 14:14–20.

Jesus instructs His disciples to "Stand" and to "Overcome" and to be "Faithful unto Death". Therefore, it is important for a disciple of Jesus to understand this Bible Truth:

> **TRIBULATION** and **PERSECUTION**
> come from our **STAND**
> on the **WORD of GOD** and our **TESTIMONY of JESUS**.

As we read the first three verses of the Book of Revelation, it is easy to see that Jesus definitely wants us to understand the actual biblical sequence of these end-time events. God shows everything to Jesus, who sends His angel to show everything to His servant John, who writes a book, so that we—even two thousand years later—can read and understand the actual biblical sequence of these end-time events. Jesus wants us to understand!

> The Revelation of Jesus Christ, which God gave Him [Jesus] to show His servants—things which must shortly take place. And He [Jesus] sent and signified it by His angel to His servant John, who bore witness to the Word of God, and to the Testimony of Jesus Christ, to all things that he saw.
>
> Blessed is he who reads and those who hear the words of this prophecy, and keep those things which are written in it; for the time is near. (Revelation 1:1–3)

CHAPTER 3

The Holy Spirit Wants Us to Understand

Let's take a closer look at this concept of what God calls "Persistent Unfaithfulness".

If we can understand how and why God chose to use an over 2,500-year period to deal with the "Persistent Unfaithfulness of Israel", then perhaps we can understand how and why God has chosen to use a seven-year period—which we call the "Seven-year Tribulation"—to deal with the "Persistent Unfaithfulness of the World".

If we can understand that, then perhaps we can understand how and why Jesus is able to count on His disciples to "not stumble" in the midst of Tribulation and Persecution.

Jesus instructs His disciples to "Stand" and to "Overcome" and to be "Faithful unto Death". Therefore, it is important for a disciple of Jesus to understand this Bible Truth:

> **TRIBULATION** and **PERSECUTION**
> come from our **STAND**
> on the **WORD of GOD** and our **TESTIMONY of JESUS**.

There is a parable in Ezekiel where God discusses "Persistent Unfaithfulness".

> Then the Word of the LORD came to me, saying: "Son of man, how is the wood of the vine better than any other

wood, the vine branch which is among the trees of the forest? Is wood taken from it to make any object? Or can men make a peg from it to hang any vessel on?

"Instead, it is thrown into the fire for fuel; the fire devours both ends of it, and its middle is burned. Is it useful for any work?

"Indeed, when it was whole, no object could be made from it. How much less will it be useful for any work when the fire has devoured it, and it is burned?"

Therefore thus says the LORD GOD: "Like the wood of the vine among the trees of the forest, which I have given to the fire for fuel, so will I give up the inhabitants of Jerusalem; and I will set My face against them.

"They will go out from one fire, but another fire shall devour them. Then you shall know that I am the LORD, when I set My face against them. Thus I will make the land desolate, because they have <u>persisted in unfaithfulness</u> [Persistent Unfaithfulness]," says the LORD GOD. (Ezekiel 15:1–8)

God also speaks of "Persistent Unfaithfulness" in Chapter 14 of Ezekiel. In this same chapter, in addition to discussing "Persistent Unfaithfulness", God also refers to His "Four Severe Judgments"—the sword, famine, wild beast, and pestilence. God starts out by saying basically, "If I sent just one judgment—just one of My 'Four Severe Judgments'—that would be enough to determine who would be faithful [Faithful unto Death]." I will underline a few words.

The word of the LORD came again to me, saying: "Son of man, when a land sins against Me by <u>persistent unfaithfulness</u> [Persistent Unfaithfulness], I will stretch out My hand against it;

"I will cut off its supply of bread, send <u>famine</u> ["Famine" is one of God's "Four Severe Judgments"] on it, and cut off man and beast from it. Even if these three men, Noah, Daniel, and Job, were in it, they would deliver only themselves by their righteousness," says the Lord God.

"If I cause <u>wild beasts</u> ["Wild Beasts" are one of God's "Four Severe Judgments"] to pass through the land, and they empty it, and make it so desolate that no man may pass through because of the beasts, even though these three men were in it, as I live," says the Lord God, "they would deliver neither sons nor daughters; only they would be delivered, and the land would be desolate.

"Or if I bring a <u>sword</u> ["The Sword" is one of God's "Four Severe Judgments"] on that land, and say, 'Sword, go through the land,' and I cut off man and beast from it, even though these three men were in it, as I live," says the Lord God, "they would deliver neither sons nor daughters, but only they themselves would be delivered.

"Or if I send a <u>pestilence</u> ["Pestilence" is one of God's "Four Severe Judgments"] into that land and pour out My fury on it in blood, and cut off from it man and beast, even though Noah, Daniel, and Job were in it, as I live," says the Lord God, "they would deliver neither son nor daughter; they would deliver only themselves by their righteousness."

For thus says the Lord God: "<u>How much more</u> it shall be when I send My <u>four severe judgments</u> ["Four Severe Judgments"] on Jerusalem—the sword and famine and wild beasts and pestilence—to cut off man and beast from it?

"<u>Yet behold, there shall be left in it a remnant who will be brought out</u>, both sons and daughters; surely they will come out to you, and you will see their ways and their doings.

"<u>Then you will be comforted</u> concerning the disaster that I have brought upon Jerusalem, all that I have brought upon it.

"<u>And they will comfort you</u>, when you see their ways and their doings; and you shall know that I have done nothing <u>without cause</u> that I have done in it," says the Lord God." (Ezekiel 14:12–23)

Prior to 1948, as a result of the "Persistent Unfaithfulness of Israel", God caused Israel to endure over 2,500 years of Tribulation and Persecution—over 2,500 years of His "Four Severe Judgments"—over 2,500 years of the sword, famine, wild beasts, and pestilence—as punishment for the "Persistent Unfaithfulness of Israel".

In the final seven years of Daniel's seventy sevens vision, as a result of the "Persistent Unfaithfulness of the World", God will cause the world to endure seven years of Tribulation and Persecution—seven years of His "Four Severe Judgments"—seven years of the sword, famine, wild beasts, and pestilence—as punishment for the "Persistent Unfaithfulness of the World".

But God still has promises to keep to Israel.

Therefore, during that same seven-year period—which we call the "Seven-year Tribulation"—God will keep ALL of His promises to Israel.

During the first three and a half years of the "Seven-year Tribulation", God will "handpick" and "set apart" and "seal" 144,000—12,000 each from the twelve tribes of Israel. These are "selected" and "set apart" and "sealed"—but they are not yet "Saved"—they are not yet disciples of Jesus.

God will use the Fifth Trumpet (the five-month torment on all but the 144,000) to make a distinction between the 144,000 and all others. Revelation 9:5 states, "In those days, men will seek death and will not find it; they will desire to die, and death will flee from them." All of this will happen during the first three and a half years of the "Seven-year Tribulation".

Then during the Sixth Trumpet—during the second three and a half years of the "Seven-year Tribulation"—God will send the two witnesses—His Two Prophets discussed in Revelation 11:1–14—and they will teach "Jesus is the Messiah" to the 144,000—from the Temple in Jerusalem—for three and a half years.

During the 1,260-day (three and a half year) ministry of the Two Prophets, every single one of the 144,000 will be saved—12,000 each from the twelve tribes of Israel will be saved—and every single one will become a disciple of Jesus. In fact, every single one of these 144,000 will be "Faithful unto Death" and we will see them in heaven—<u>prior to the Rapture</u>—and they are described as "ones who follow the Lamb wherever He goes" (Revelation 14:1–5).

All of this will happen during the Sixth Trumpet—during the second three and a half years of the "Seven-year Tribulation". Therefore, Israel will be saved—and God's promise to save Israel will be fulfilled—and all of this will occur <u>prior to the Rapture</u>.

God has promised that "Israel will be saved". Nevertheless, Israel must be "saved" the same way any person is "saved".

Paul taught that an individual is saved by grace through faith. Consider Ephesians 2:8–9: "For by grace you have been saved through faith, and that not of yourselves; it is the gift of God, not of works, lest anyone should boast."

In Romans, Paul taught the following.

> But what does it [the Scripture] say? "The word is near you, in your mouth and in your heart" (that is, the word of faith which we preach): that if you confess with your mouth the Lord Jesus and believe in your heart that God has raised Him from the dead, you will be saved.
>
> For with the heart one believes unto righteousness, and with the mouth confession is made unto salvation.
>
> For the Scripture says, "Whoever believes on Him will not be put to shame."
>
> <u>For there is no distinction between Jew and Greek</u> [Israel must be saved the same way any person is saved], for the same Lord over all is rich to all who call upon Him.

For "whoever calls on the name of the Lord shall be Saved."

How then shall they call on Him in whom they have not believed?

And how shall they believe in Him of whom they have not heard?

And how shall they hear without a preacher?

And how shall they preach unless they are sent?

As it is written:

"How beautiful are the feet of those who preach the gospel of peace,

Who bring glad tidings of good things!"

But they have not all obeyed the gospel. For Isaiah says, "Lord, who has believed our report?"

So then Faith comes by hearing, and hearing by the Word of God. (Romans 10:8–17).

When God sends the two witnesses [His Two Prophets] to the Temple in Jerusalem for 1,260 days [three and a half years], God will give them incredible power, including the ability to strike the earth will all plagues as often as they desire. These Two Prophets will teach "Jesus is the Messiah" to the 144,000 at the Temple in Jerusalem. Nevertheless, God will wait until after the Antichrist has <u>Stopped the Daily Sacrifices at the Temple</u> before He sends His Two Prophets.

By arriving at the Temple just after the Antichrist has stopped the "Daily Sacrifices", the power of these Two Prophets will be sufficient to prevent the Antichrist from entering the Temple and committing the "Abomination of Desolation" at that time. In fact, the power of these Two

Prophets will be enough to prevent the Antichrist from committing the "Abomination of Desolation" at any time during their 1,260-day [three and a half year] ministry.

We will see later in the book of Daniel that there are actually 1,290 days from the time that the Antichrist stops the "Daily Sacrifices" until the day the Antichrist enters the Temple and commits the "Abomination of Desolation".

The Two Prophets will teach "Jesus is the Messiah" to the 144,000 at the Temple in Jerusalem. Therefore, let's look at how Jesus ministered to His disciples—after He rose from the dead—before He ascended to heaven—during His first coming.

> Then He said to them, "O foolish ones, and slow of heart to believe in all that the prophets [the Old Testament prophets] have spoken! Ought not the Christ [the Messiah] to have suffered these things and to enter into His glory?"
>
> And beginning at Moses and all the Prophets [the entire Old Testament], He expounded to them in all the Scriptures [the Old Testament Scriptures] the things concerning Himself [the Messiah]. (Luke 24:25–27)

The Two Prophets will teach "Jesus is the Messiah" to the 144,000 at the Temple in Jerusalem—and they will do exactly what Jesus did—they will begin with Moses and all the Prophets [the Old Testament Prophets] and expound to them in all the Scriptures [the Old Testament Scriptures] the things concerning the Messiah [Jesus].

Look at another time that Jesus ministered to His disciples—after he had risen from the dead—just before He ascended to heaven—during His first coming.

> Then He said to them, "These are the words which I spoke to you while I was still with you, that all things must be fulfilled which were written in the Law of Moses and the Prophets and the Psalms [the entire Old Testament] concerning Me [the Messiah]."

> And He opened their understanding, that they might comprehend the Scriptures [the Old Testament Scriptures concerning the Messiah].
>
> Then He said to them, "Thus it is written, and thus it was necessary for the Christ [the Messiah] to suffer and to rise from the dead the third day, and that repentance and remission of sins should be preached in His name to all nations, beginning at Jerusalem.
>
> And you are witnesses of these things. Behold, I send the Promise of My Father upon you; but tarry in the city of Jerusalem until you are endued with power from on high." (Luke 24:44–49)

The Two Prophets will teach "Jesus is the Messiah" to the 144,000 at the Temple in Jerusalem—and they will do exactly what Jesus did—they will begin with the Law of Moses and the Prophets and the Psalms [the entire Old Testament] and they will open the understanding of the 144,000 so that they might comprehend the Scriptures [the entire Old Testament Scriptures] concerning the Messiah [Jesus].

God has promised that "Israel will be saved".

> Isaiah also cries out concerning Israel: "Though the number of the children of Israel be as the sand of the sea, the remnant will be saved [Israel will be saved]." (Romans 9:27)

God has promised that "Israel will be saved".

> And so all Israel will be saved, as it is written: "The Deliverer will come out of Zion, and He will turn away ungodliness from Jacob; For this is My covenant with them, when I take away their sins." [Israel will be saved] (Romans 11:26–27)

As God prophesied through Ezekiel, once we see that Israel is saved, we will understand and be comforted.

> "<u>Then you will be comforted</u> concerning the disaster that I have brought upon Jerusalem, all that I have brought on it. <u>And they will comfort you</u>, when you see their ways and their doings; and you shall know that I have done nothing <u>without cause</u> that I have done it," says the LORD GOD. (Ezekiel 14:12–23)

God has promised that "Israel will be saved". Nevertheless, Israel must be "saved" the same way any person is "saved".

> But what does it [the Scripture] say? "The WORD is near you, in your Mouth and in your Heart"—that is the Word of Faith which we preach—that if you confess with your mouth the Lord Jesus and believe in your heart that God has raised Him from the dead, you will be saved. For with the heart one believes unto Righteousness and with the mouth confession is made unto Salvation.
>
> For the Scripture says, "Whoever believes on Him will not be put to shame." <u>For there is no distinction between Jew and Greek</u> [Israel must be saved the same way any person is saved], for the same Lord over all is rich to all who call upon Him. For "Whoever calls on the name of the Lord shall be Saved." (Romans 10:8–13)

We will see in Revelation how God will fulfill ALL of His promises to Israel during the last seven years, but before we do that, let's go back to the book of Daniel.

> Then he shall confirm a covenant with many for one week [one seven or one seven-year period or 7 years]; but in the middle of the week [in the middle of this seven-year covenant with many] he [the Antichrist] shall bring an end to sacrifice and offering [after three and a half years, the Antichrist will break the covenant and <u>Stop the Daily Sacrifices at the Temple</u>]. And on the wing of abominations shall be one who makes desolate, even

until the consummation, which is determined, is poured out on the desolate. (Daniel 9:20–27)

This passage of Scripture is just one of the many Scriptures in the book of Daniel that show that the Antichrist will enter Jerusalem with a small army and Stop the Daily Sacrifices at the Temple.

In fact, when the Antichrist stops the Daily Sacrifices at the Temple, this event is actually the "starting point" of a countdown for four important end-time events. Consider this event as day 0.

- After day 0—in other words, after the Antichrist has Stopped the Daily Sacrifices at the Temple—then the two witnesses [the Two Prophets] will appear and will minister to the 144,000 for 1,260 days. They will teach "Jesus is the Messiah" to the 144,000 at the Temple in Jerusalem for three and a half years.
- On day 1,290—in other words, one thousand two hundred and ninety days after the Antichrist has Stopped the Daily Sacrifices at the Temple—the Antichrist will enter the Holy of Holies in the Temple and commit the "Abomination of Desolation".
- On day 1,335—in other words, one thousand three hundred and thirty-five days after the Antichrist has Stopped the Daily Sacrifices at the Temple—the Bible says that he who waits and comes to the one thousand three hundred and thirty-five days will be "Blessed". When we subtract 1,290 from 1,335, we can understand that this event will occur approximately 45 days after the "Abomination of Desolation" [which occurs inside the Temple]. This event appears to be the exact same event that Jesus referred to in Matthew 24:15–22, Mark 13:14–20, Matthew 24:29–31, and Mark 13:24–27. This event is known as the "Rapture".
- On day 2,300—in other words, two thousand three hundred days after the Antichrist has Stopped the Daily Sacrifices at the Temple—the Sanctuary [the Temple] will be cleansed. This would certainly happen when Jesus begins to rule on the earth for 1,000 years from Jerusalem. This event will occur after the Battle of Armageddon is over—after the Seventh Bowl of the "Wrath of God" has been poured out onto an unsaved world. When we subtract 1,335 from 2,300, we can understand that

the "Wrath of God" will last approximately 965 days—almost three years.

Let's look at another prophetic Scripture in Daniel that refers to when the Antichrist will <u>Stop the Daily Sacrifices at the Temple</u>. In this passage, an angel is explaining one of the visions that Daniel has seen that refers to the "time of the end".

> "But you, Daniel, shut up the words, and seal the book until <u>the time of the end</u>; many shall run to and fro, and knowledge shall increase."
>
> Then I, Daniel, looked; and there stood two others, one on this riverbank and the other on that riverbank.
>
> And one said to the man clothed in linen, who was above the waters of the river, "<u>How long shall the fulfillment of these wonders be?</u>"
>
> Then I heard the man clothed in linen, who was above the waters of the river, when he held up his right hand and his left hand to heaven, and swore by Him who lives forever, that it shall be for a time, times, and half a time [three and a half years]; and when the power of the holy people has been completely shattered, all these things shall be finished.
>
> Although I heard, I did not understand.
>
> Then I said, "<u>My lord, what shall be the end of these things?</u>"
>
> And he said, "Go your way, Daniel, for the words are closed up and sealed till the time of the end.
>
> "Many shall be purified, made white, and refined, but the wicked shall do wickedly; none of the wicked shall understand, but the wise shall understand.

"And from the time that the '<u>Daily Sacrifice</u>' is taken away,

and

"the '<u>Abomination of Desolation</u>' is set up,

"There shall be one thousand two hundred and ninety days [<u>1,290 days</u>].

"<u>Blessed</u> is he who waits, and comes to the one thousand three hundred and thirty-five days [<u>1,335 days</u>].

"But you, go your way till the end; for you shall rest, and will arise to your inheritance at the end of the days." (Daniel 12:4–13)

Let's look at another prophetic Scripture in Daniel that refers to when the Antichrist will <u>Stop the Daily Sacrifices at the Temple</u>.

> And out of one of them came a little horn [the Antichrist] which grew exceedingly great toward the south, toward the east, and toward the Glorious Land [Israel]. And it grew up to the host of heaven; and it cast down some of the host and some of the stars to the ground, and trampled them. He even exalted himself as high as the Prince of the host; and by him [the Antichrist] the daily sacrifices [the Daily Sacrifices at the Temple] were taken away, and the place of His sanctuary was cast down.
>
> Because of transgression, an army was given over to the horn [the Antichrist] to oppose the daily sacrifices [the Daily Sacrifices at the Temple]; and he cast truth down to the ground. He did all this and prospered."
>
> Then I heard a holy one speaking; and another holy one said to that certain one who was speaking, "How long

will the vision be, concerning the daily sacrifices [the Daily Sacrifices at the Temple] and the transgression of desolation, the giving of both the sanctuary [the Temple] and the host to be trampled underfoot?"

And he said to me, "For two thousand three hundred days [2,300 days—literally 2,300 "evenings and mornings"]; then the sanctuary [the Temple] shall be cleansed."

Then it happened, when I, Daniel, had seen the vision and was seeking the meaning, that suddenly there stood before me one having the appearance of a man. And I heard a man's voice between the banks of the Ulai, who called, and said, "Gabriel, make this man understand the vision." So he came near where I stood, and when he came I was afraid and fell on my face; but he [Gabriel] said to me, "Understand, son of man, that the vision refers to the time of the end."

Now, as he [Gabriel] was speaking with me, I was in a deep sleep with my face to the ground; but he [Gabriel] touched me, and stood me upright. And he [Gabriel] said, "Look, I am making known to you what shall happen in the latter time of the indignation; for at the appointed time the end shall be.

"The ram which you saw, having the two horns—they are the kings of Media and Persia. And the male goat is the kingdom of Greece. The large horn that is between its eyes is the first king. As for the broken horn and the four that stood up in its place, four kingdoms shall arise out of that nation, but not with its power.

"And in the latter time of their kingdom,
When the transgressors have reached their fullness,
A king shall arise [the Antichrist],
Having fierce features,
Who understands sinister schemes.

"His power shall be mighty, but not by his own power;
He shall destroy fearfully,
And shall prosper and thrive;
He [the Antichrist] shall destroy the mighty, and also the holy people.

"Through his cunning
He [the Antichrist] shall cause deceit to prosper under his rule;
And he shall exalt himself in his heart.
He shall destroy many in their prosperity.
He shall even rise against the Prince of princes;
But he [the Antichrist] shall be broken without human means.

"And the vision of the evenings and mornings
Which was told is true [the vision of the 2,300 days is true—in other words, the vision of the 2,300 evenings and mornings is true. This is the time period that begins when the Antichrist <u>Stops the Daily Sacrifices at the Temple</u> and ends with the <u>Temple being cleansed</u>. This event of "Cleansing the Temple" would certainly take place when the "Wrath of God" is over and when Jesus begins to rule from Jerusalem for 1,000 years];

Therefore seal up the vision,
For it refers to many days in the future."

And I, Daniel, fainted and was sick for days; afterward I arose and went about the king's business. I was astonished by the vision, but no one understood it. (Daniel 8:9–27)

As mentioned earlier, because the Temple was destroyed in AD 70, these end-time events have always been hard to understand. Hopefully you can see that prior to Israel becoming a nation (again) in 1948, the biblical sequence of events described in the teachings of Jesus and described in the teachings of Paul, and the sequence of events showed to

Daniel in the Book of Daniel, and the sequence of events showed to John in the Book of Revelation were simply hard to understand, because they all mentioned the Temple, and for almost two thousand years prior to 1948, there has been no Temple. Therefore it was tough for folks to simply understand and believe that "What the Bible Said" was actually true.

Please understand:

My Job is NOT to convince you that the Bible is True.

My Job is to Teach you What the Bible Says.

It is the Holy Spirit's Job to convince you that the Bible is True.

Putting the entire sequence together, we get a clear picture of "What Does the Bible Say?" This is the actual biblical "<u>Sequence of Events</u>" that we have seen so far.

- Jesus, the Messiah, accomplishes what He was sent to the earth to accomplish during His first coming: "For God so loved the world that He gave His only begotten Son, that whoever believes in Him should not perish but have everlasting life" (John 3:16).
- You and I now have the opportunity to become disciples of Jesus.

> But what does it [the Scripture] say? "The WORD is near you, in your Mouth and in your Heart"—that is the Word of Faith which we preach—that if you confess with your mouth the Lord Jesus and believe in your heart that God has raised Him from the dead—you will be Saved. For with the heart one believes unto Righteousness, and with the mouth confession is made unto Salvation. (Romans 10:8–10)

- Jesus commands His disciples to be "Faithful unto Death"— Matthew 16:25; Mark 8:35; Luke 9:24; John 12:25.
- Beginnings of Sorrows—This could have begun as early as when Jesus ascended to heaven because there certainly have been wars, rumors of wars, earthquakes, etc. since that time—Matthew 24:3–13; Mark 13:3–13.
- The disciples of Jesus began to be persecuted and were "Faithful unto Death".

> And they stoned Stephen as he was calling on God and saying, "Lord Jesus, receive my spirit." Then he knelt down and cried out with a loud voice, "Lord, do not charge them with this sin." And when he had said this, he fell asleep. Now Saul [who later became the great "Apostle Paul"] was consenting to his death. At that time a great persecution arose against the church which was at Jerusalem; and they were all scattered throughout the regions of Judea and Samaria, except the apostles. And devout men carried Stephen to his burial, and made great lamentation over him. As for Saul, he made havoc of the church, entering every house, and dragging off men and women, committing them to prison. Therefore those who were scattered went everywhere preaching the WORD. (Acts 7:59–8:4)

- The Temple and Jerusalem are destroyed in AD 70 by the Roman Empire; over one million are killed, and the children of Israel are scattered throughout the earth in exile and without a homeland. Israel ceases to exist as a nation for almost 2,000 years.
- The children of Israel continue to endure God's "Four Severe Judgments"—the sword, famine, wild beasts, and pestilence. Israel endures over 2,500 years of God's punishment for the iniquity of the nation of Israel beginning with its seventy-year captivity in Babylon during the time of Daniel and continuing through the years of the World War II Holocaust—which ended in 1945. Israel endures over 2,500 years of God's punishment for the "Persistent Unfaithfulness of Israel"—Ezekiel 4:1–6; Leviticus 26:18–28.
- Israel becomes a nation (again) in 1948; that ends the over 2,500 years of God's punishment for the "Persistent Unfaithfulness of Israel". God honors His promise and returns Israel to its homeland in 1948.

At some point in the future,

- God takes the Scroll in His right hand; He is ready to start the final seven years and fulfill ALL of His promises to Israel—Revelation 5:1; Daniel 9:20–27.

- There is a seven-year covenant with many—which may give the nation of Israel an opportunity to rebuild the Temple (if the Temple has not already been rebuilt by that time)—Daniel 9:20–27.
- Jesus opens the First Seal to start the "Seven-year Tribulation"—Revelation 6:1.
- Tribulation begins and continues—Matthew 24:3–13.
- The "Seven-year Tribulation" is God's punishment for the "Persistent Unfaithfulness of the World". This is seven years of what God calls His "Four Severe Judgments"—the sword, famine, wild beasts, and pestilence. Since Christians are in the world, Christians will experience what the world experiences and Christians will endure what the world endures—during the Tribulation.
- God will use these final seven years to fulfill ALL of His promises to Israel—Daniel 9:20–27.
- Temple is rebuilt—the Bible does not tell us whether the Temple is rebuilt before the Tribulation begins, but the Temple is definitely rebuilt before the Antichrist commits the Abomination of Desolation—Matthew 24:15–22; Mark 13:14–20; 2 Thessalonians 2:1–5.
- Israel starts the Daily Sacrifices—Daniel 9:20–27.
- The Antichrist enters Jerusalem with an army and <u>Stops the Daily Sacrifices at the Temple</u>—Daniel 9:20–27. This event is the "starting point" of a countdown for four important end-time events. Consider this event as day 0.
- After day 0—in other words, after the Antichrist has <u>Stopped the Daily Sacrifices at the Temple</u>, the two witnesses [the Two Prophets] will appear and will minister to the 144,000 for 1,260 days. They will teach "Jesus is the Messiah" to the 144,000 at the Temple in Jerusalem for three and a half years.
- On day 1,290—in other words, one thousand two hundred and ninety days after the Antichrist has <u>Stopped the Daily Sacrifices at the Temple</u>—the Antichrist will enter the Holy of Holies in the Temple and commit the "Abomination of Desolation"—Daniel 12:4-13.
- Abomination of Desolation—Daniel 12:4-13; Matthew 24:15–22; Mark 13:14–20; 2 Thessalonians 2:1–5.

- Great Tribulation—In Matthew 24:21–22, Jesus said, "For then there will be <u>Great Tribulation</u>, such as has not been since the beginning of the world until this time, no, nor ever shall be. And unless those days were shortened, no flesh would be saved; but for the elect's sake those days will be shortened."
- In Matthew, Jesus referred to the time toward the end of the Tribulation as the "Great Tribulation". This is the time immediately after the Abomination of Desolation and just before the Rapture—Matthew 24:15–22; Mark 13:14–20; Matthew 24:29–31; Mark 13:24–27.
- Sun and moon are darkened—Matthew 24:29–31; Mark 13:24–27.
- Last Trumpet—1 Corinthians 15:51–52.
- Jesus descends from heaven with a shout, with the voice of an archangel, and with the Trumpet of God—1 Thessalonians 4:15–18.
- Son of Man coming on the clouds—Matthew 24:29–31; Mark 13:24–27; Revelation 14:14–20.
- On day 1,335—in other words, one thousand three hundred and thirty-five days after the Antichrist has <u>Stopped the Daily Sacrifices at the Temple</u>—the Bible says that he who waits and comes to the one thousand three hundred and thirty-five days will be "Blessed". When we subtract 1,290 from 1,335, we can understand that this event will occur approximately 45 days after the "Abomination of Desolation" [which occurs inside the Temple]. This event appears to be the exact same event that Jesus referred to in Matthew 24:15–22, Mark 13:14–20, Matthew 24:29–31, and Mark 13:24–27. This event is known as the "Rapture"—Daniel 12:4-13.
- Rapture—Matthew 24:15–22; Mark 13:14–20; Matthew 24:29–31; Mark 13:24–27; 1 Corinthians 15:51–52; 1 Thessalonians 4:15–18; Revelation 14:14–20.
- Wrath of God—Revelation 14:14–20.
- On day 2,300—in other words, two thousand three hundred days after the Antichrist has <u>Stopped the Daily Sacrifices at the Temple</u>—the Sanctuary [the Temple] will be cleansed [<u>The Temple will be cleansed</u>]. This would certainly happen when Jesus begins to rule on the earth for 1,000 years from Jerusalem.

This event will occur after the Battle of Armageddon is over—after the last bowl of the "Wrath of God" has been poured out onto an unsaved world. When we subtract 1,335 from 2,300, we can understand that the "Wrath of God" will last approximately 965 days—almost three years—Daniel 12:4-13.

- Jesus begins to rule on the earth for 1,000 years from Jerusalem.

Jesus instructs His disciples to "Stand" and to "Overcome" and to be "Faithful unto Death". Therefore, it is important for a disciple of Jesus to understand this Bible Truth:

> **TRIBULATION** and **PERSECUTION**
> come from our **STAND**
> on the **WORD of GOD** and our **TESTIMONY of JESUS**.

As we read the first three verses of the Book of Revelation, it is easy to see that the Holy Spirit definitely wants us to understand the actual biblical sequence of these end-time events. God shows everything to Jesus, who sends His angel to show everything to His servant John, who writes a book, so that we—even two thousand years later—can read and understand the actual biblical sequence of these end-time events. The Holy Spirit wants us to understand!

> The Revelation of Jesus Christ, which God gave Him [Jesus] to show His servants—things which must shortly take place. And He [Jesus] sent and signified it by His angel to His servant John, who bore witness to the Word of God, and to the Testimony of Jesus Christ, to all things that he saw.
>
> Blessed is he who reads and those who hear the words of this prophecy, and keep those things which are written in it; for the time is near. (Revelation 1:1–3)

CHAPTER 4

Understanding the Final Seven Years–Part 1

According to Revelation, there will come a time when God will take a certain Scroll in His right hand. An angel will ask, "Who is worthy to open the Scroll and to loose its Seals?" (Revelation 5:2). That will be God's way of saying that He is ready to start the final seven years and to fulfill ALL of His promises to Israel.

As mentioned earlier, when John saw Jesus take the Scroll from the hand of God, there were Seven Seals, and Seven Thunders, and Seven Trumpets, and Seven Bowls of Wrath. These Seven Bowls of Wrath are the <u>Wrath of God</u>. Therefore it is important to understand that there is a major difference between the <u>Tribulation</u> and the <u>Wrath of God</u>.

What we call the "<u>Seven-year Tribulation</u>" has to do with the Seven Seals, and the Seven Thunders, and the Seven Trumpets. What the Bible calls the "<u>Wrath of God</u>" has to do with the Seven Bowls of Wrath. Throughout scripture, the sequence of end-time events that the Bible teaches is this.

- Tribulation.
- Rapture.
- Wrath of God.

Before we look at what Revelation says about the final seven years, let's look at what Jesus said to His disciples in the first three chapters of Revelation—encouraging them to "Understand" and to be "Faithful unto Death".

> He who has an ear, let him hear [Understand] what the Spirit says to the churches. To him who overcomes [Faithful unto Death] I will give to eat from the Tree of Life, which is in the midst of the Paradise of God. (Revelation 2:7)

This is repeated six more times for emphasis.

> Do not fear any of those things which you are about to suffer. Indeed, the devil is about to throw some of you into prison, that you may be tested, and you will have tribulation ten days. Be faithful unto death, and I will give you the crown of life. He who has an ear, let him hear [Understand] what the Spirit says to the churches. He who overcomes [Faithful unto Death] shall not be hurt by the second death. (Revelation 2:10–11)

> He who has an ear, let him hear [Understand] what the Spirit says to the churches. To him who overcomes [Faithful unto Death] I will give some of the hidden manna to eat. And I will give him a white stone, and on the stone a new name written which no one knows except him who receives it. (Revelation 2:17)

> And he who overcomes [Faithful unto Death], and keeps My works until the end [Faithful unto Death], to him I will give power over the nations—"He shall rule them with a rod of iron: They shall be dashed to pieces like the potter's vessels"—as I have also received from My Father; and I will give him the morning star. He who has an ear, let him hear [Understand] what the Spirit says to the churches. (Revelation 2:26–29)

> He who overcomes [Faithful unto Death] shall be clothed in white garments, and I will not blot out his name from the Book of Life; but I will confess his name before My Father and before His angels. He who has an ear, let him

hear [Understand] what the Spirit says to the churches. (Revelation 3:5–6)

He who overcomes [Faithful unto Death], I will make him a pillar in the Temple of My God, and he shall go out no more. I will write on him the name of My God and the name of the city of My God, the New Jerusalem, which comes down out of heaven from My God. And I will write on him My new name. He who has an ear, let him hear [Understand] what the Spirit says to the churches. (Revelation 3:12–13)

To him who overcomes [Faithful unto Death] I will grant to sit with Me on My throne, as I also overcame and sat down with My Father on His throne [Jesus was Faithful unto Death]. He who has an ear, let him hear [Understand] what the Spirit says to the churches. (Revelation 3:21–22)

In Revelation 12:11, the Bible gives us instructions on exactly how to overcome.

And they overcame him [Satan] by <u>the Blood of the Lamb</u> and by <u>the Word of their Testimony</u>, and <u>they did not love their lives to the death</u> [Faithful unto Death].

This concept of being "Faithful unto Death" that Jesus taught His disciples in Revelation is consistent with what Jesus taught His disciples during His first coming.

For whoever desires to save his life will lose it, but whoever loses his life for My sake will find it [Faithful unto Death]. (Matthew 16:25)

For whoever desires to save his life will lose it, but whoever loses his life for My sake and the gospel's will save it [Faithful unto Death]. (Mark 8:35)

> For whoever desires to save his life will lose it, but whoever loses his life for My sake will save it [Faithful unto Death]. (Luke 9:24)

> He who loves his life will lose it, and he who hates his life in this world will keep it for eternal life [Faithful unto Death]. (John 12:25)

Revelation 3:10–11 is often misunderstood. I will underline a few words.

> Because you have kept My command to persevere, I also will keep you from the <u>hour of trial</u> which shall come upon the whole earth, to test those who dwell on the earth. Behold, I am coming quickly! Hold fast what you have, that no one may take your crown. (Revelation 3:10–11)

This <u>hour of trial</u> [mentioned in Revelation 3:10] is often taught as being the <u>Tribulation</u>, inferring that Jesus will keep these disciples from having to go through the <u>Tribulation</u>. Nevertheless, the sequence of end-time events that the Bible teaches is this.

- Tribulation
- Rapture
- Wrath of God

The <u>hour of trial</u> [mentioned in Revelation 3:10] refers to the <u>Seven Bowls of Wrath</u> [Wrath of God]. The Wrath of God occurs <u>after</u> the Rapture and will be poured out onto an unsaved world—upon the whole earth—to test those who dwell on the earth.

In Revelation 3:10–11, Jesus was saying, "Be Faithful unto Death" [and overcome that way] or "Be Faithful until the Rapture" [and overcome that way]. But either way, Jesus was saying, "If you keep My command to persevere [If you keep My command to be Faithful unto Death], I will keep you from the hour of trial [I will keep you from the Wrath of God]."

Revelation 3:10-11 should be read like this.

> Because you have kept My command to persevere [because you have kept My command to be Faithful unto Death], I also will keep you from the hour of trial [I also will keep you from the Wrath of God] which shall come upon the whole earth, to test those who dwell on the earth. Behold, I am coming quickly [Behold the Rapture is coming quickly]! Hold fast what you have [Be Faithful unto Death], that no one may take your crown. (Revelation 3:10–11)

The Bible truth is that disciples of Jesus do not go through the Wrath of God and the sequence of end-time events that the Bible teaches is this.

- Tribulation
- Rapture
- Wrath of God

As mentioned earlier, in Revelation we will see Jesus take the Scroll from the hand of God and open it in the following order:

1. The Seven Seals.
2. The First Four Trumpets.
3. The Fifth Trumpet (the First Woe).
4. The Sixth Trumpet (the Second Woe).
   Both the Seven Thunders and the three and a half year [1,260 days] Ministry of the Two Prophets occur during the period of the Sixth Trumpet.
5. The Seventh Trumpet (the Third Woe).
   Some amazing things happen at the Seventh Trumpet, including an Angel Preaching the Gospel to those on the earth prior to the Rapture. The Rapture occurs during the time of the Seventh Trumpet. Then after the Rapture occurs, the Seven Bowls of the Wrath of God are poured out onto an unsaved world.
6. The Seven Bowls of the Wrath of God.

Let's look at what Revelation says about the final seven years. In this chapter, we will look at the first half of what we call the "Seven-year

Tribulation" and in the next chapter we will look at the second half of the "Seven-year Tribulation".

In Revelation 5:1, God takes the Scroll in His right hand.

> And I saw in the right hand of Him who sat on the throne a scroll written inside and on the back, sealed with seven seals.

In Revelation 5:7, Jesus takes the Scroll.

> Then He [Jesus] came and took the scroll out of the right hand of Him [God] who sat on the throne.

In Revelation 6:1–8, Jesus opens the first Four Seals.

> Now I saw when the Lamb [Jesus] opened one of the seals [First Seal]; and I heard one of the four living creatures saying with a voice like thunder, "Come and see." And I looked, and behold, a white horse. He who sat on it had a bow; and a crown was given to him, and he went out conquering and to conquer.

> When He [Jesus] opened the second seal [Second Seal], I heard the second living creature saying, "Come and see." Another horse, fiery red, went out. And it was granted to the one who sat on it to take peace from the earth, and that people should kill one another; and there was given to him a great sword.

> When He [Jesus] opened the third seal [Third Seal], I heard the third living creature say, "Come and see." So I looked, and behold, a black horse, and he who sat on it had a pair of scales in his hand. And I heard a voice in the midst of the four living creatures saying, "A quart of wheat for a denarius, and three quarts of barley for a denarius; and do not harm the oil and the wine."

> When He [Jesus] opened the fourth seal [Fourth Seal], I heard the voice of the fourth living creature saying, "Come and see." So I looked, and behold, a pale horse. And the name of him who sat on it was Death, and Hades followed with him. And power was given to them over a fourth of the earth, to kill with sword, with hunger, with death, and by the beasts of the earth [This is what the Bible calls "God's Four Severe Judgments"—the sword, famine, wild beasts, and pestilence].

In Revelation 6:9–11, Jesus opens the Fifth Seal.

> When He [Jesus] opened the fifth seal [Fifth Seal], I saw under the altar [in heaven] the souls of those who had been slain [killed] for the Word of God and for the Testimony which they held [Tribulation and Persecution come from our Stand on the Word of God and our Testimony of Jesus].
>
> And they cried with a loud voice, saying, "How long, O Lord, holy and true, until You judge and avenge our blood on those who dwell on the earth?"
>
> Then a white robe was given to each of them; and it was said to them that they should rest a little while longer, until both the number of their fellow servants and their brethren, who would be killed as they were, was completed.

In Revelation 6:12–17, Jesus opens the Sixth Seal.

> I looked when He [Jesus] opened the sixth seal [Sixth Seal], and behold, there was a great earthquake; and the sun became black as sackcloth of hair, and the moon became like blood. And the stars of heaven fell to the earth, as a fig tree drops its late figs when it is shaken by a mighty wind. Then the sky receded as a scroll when it

is rolled up, and every mountain and island was moved out of its place.

And the kings of the earth, the great men, the rich men, the commanders, the mighty men, every slave and every free man, hid themselves in the caves and in the rocks of the mountains, and said to the mountains and rocks, "Fall on us and hide us from the face of Him who sits on the throne and from the wrath of the Lamb! For the great day of His wrath has come, and who is able to stand?" [Men think that this is the "Wrath of the Lamb"—but this is NOT the "Wrath of God". This is still during the first three and a half years of the "Seven-year Tribulation".]

In Revelation 7:1–17—still during the time of the Sixth Seal—John is allowed to see what happens just prior to the Seventh Seal being opened.

After these things I saw four angels standing at the four corners of the earth, holding the four winds of the earth, that the wind should not blow on the earth, on the sea, or on any tree. Then I saw another angel ascending from the east, having the seal of the living God. And he cried with a loud voice to the four angels to whom it was granted to harm the earth and the sea, saying, "Do not harm the earth, the sea, or the trees till we have sealed the servants of our God on their foreheads."

And I heard the number of those who were sealed. One hundred and forty-four thousand of all the tribes of the children of Israel were sealed [These 144,000 are 12,000 each from twelve Tribes of Israel. These 144,000 have been "hand picked" and "set apart" and "sealed"—but they are not yet "Saved"—they are not yet "Disciples of Jesus"]:

of the tribe of Judah twelve thousand were sealed;
of the tribe of Reuben twelve thousand were sealed;
of the tribe of Gad twelve thousand were sealed;

of the tribe of Asher twelve thousand were sealed;
of the tribe of Naphtali twelve thousand were sealed;
of the tribe of Manasseh twelve thousand were sealed;

of the tribe of Simeon twelve thousand were sealed;
of the tribe of Levi twelve thousand were sealed;
of the tribe of Issachar twelve thousand were sealed;

of the tribe of Zebulun twelve thousand were sealed;
of the tribe of Joseph twelve thousand were sealed;
of the tribe of Benjamin twelve thousand were sealed.

After these things I looked, and behold, a great multitude which no one could number, of all nations, tribes, peoples, and tongues, standing before the throne and before the Lamb, clothed with white robes, with palm branches in their hands, and crying out with a loud voice, saying, "Salvation belongs to our God who sits on the throne, and to the Lamb!"

All the angels stood around the throne and the elders and the four living creatures, and fell on their faces before the throne and worshiped God, saying: "Amen! Blessing and glory and wisdom,
Thanksgiving and honor and power and might,
Be to our God forever and ever.
Amen."

Then one of the elders answered, saying to me, "Who are these arrayed in white robes, and where did they come from?"

And I said to him, "Sir, you know."

So he said to me, "These are the ones who come out of the great <u>Tribulation</u>, and washed their robes and made them white in the blood of the Lamb. Therefore they are before the throne of God, and serve Him day and night in His temple. And He who sits on the throne will dwell among them.

They shall neither hunger anymore nor thirst anymore; the sun shall not strike them, nor any heat; for the Lamb who is in the midst of the throne will shepherd them and lead them to living fountains of waters. And God will wipe away every tear from their eyes." [These are the disciples of Jesus who were Faithful unto Death. When one of the elders spoke to John and referred to the first half of the Tribulation as being the "great Tribulation"—he was speaking correctly—since one fourth of the earth had just been killed during that time period—and it had definitely never been that bad before. Nevertheless, this is NOT the same time period that Jesus was referring to when He spoke of the "Great Tribulation"—because the time period that Jesus was referring to will occur after the Abomination of Desolation and just before the Rapture—and because the time period that Jesus was referring to will (not only) have never been that bad before—but it will (also) <u>never be that bad again</u>].

In Revelation 8:1–6, Jesus opens the Seventh Seal.

When He [Jesus] opened the seventh seal [Seventh Seal], there was silence in heaven for about half an hour. And I saw the seven angels who stand before God, and to them were given seven trumpets [Seven Trumpets]. Then another angel, having a golden censer, came and stood at the altar. He was given much incense, that he should offer it with the prayers of all the saints upon the golden altar which was before the throne.

And the smoke of the incense, with the prayers of the saints, ascended before God from the angel's hand. Then the angel took the censer, filled it with fire from the altar, and threw it to the earth. And there were noises, thunderings, lightnings, and an earthquake.

So the seven angels who had the seven trumpets [Seven Trumpets] prepared themselves to sound.

In Revelation 8:7–13, the first Four Trumpets sound.

The first angel sounded [First Trumpet]: And hail and fire followed, mingled with blood, and they were thrown to the earth. And a third of the trees were burned up, and all green grass was burned up.

Then the second angel sounded [Second Trumpet]: And something like a great mountain burning with fire was thrown into the sea, and a third of the sea became blood. And a third of the living creatures in the sea died, and a third of the ships were destroyed.

Then the third angel sounded [Third Trumpet]: And a great star fell from heaven, burning like a torch, and it fell on a third of the rivers and on the springs of water. The name of the star is Wormwood. A third of the waters became wormwood, and many men died from the water, because it was made bitter.

Then the fourth angel sounded [Fourth Trumpet]: And a third of the sun was struck, a third of the moon, and a third of the stars, so that a third of them were darkened. A third of the day did not shine, and likewise the night.

And I looked, and I heard an angel flying through the midst of heaven, saying with a loud voice, "<u>Woe, Woe, Woe</u> to the inhabitants of the earth, <u>because of the remaining blasts of the trumpet of the three angels who are about to sound!</u>" [The Fifth Trumpet is given the name of the "First Woe"; the Sixth Trumpet is given the name of the "Second Woe"; and the Seventh Trumpet is given the name of the "Third Woe".]

In Revelation 9:1–12, the Fifth Trumpet sounds.

> Then the fifth angel sounded [The Fifth Trumpet is given the name of the "First Woe"]: And I saw a star fallen from heaven to the earth. To him was given the key to the bottomless pit.
>
> And he opened the bottomless pit, and smoke arose out of the pit like the smoke of a great furnace. So the sun and the air were darkened because of the smoke of the pit.
>
> Then out of the smoke locusts came upon the earth. And to them was given power, as the scorpions of the earth have power.
>
> They were commanded not to harm the grass of the earth, or any green thing, or any tree, but only those men who do not have the seal of God on their foreheads [They were commanded not to harm the 144,000].
>
> And they were not given authority to kill them, but to torment them for five months. Their torment was like the torment of a scorpion when it strikes a man.
>
> In those days men will seek death and will not find it; they will desire to die, and death will flee from them [This is a five month torment—on all but the 144,000. This is a five month torment on all but the 12,000 each from twelve tribes of Israel who have been sealed by God. These 144,000 have been "hand picked" and "set apart" and "sealed"—but they are not yet "Saved"—they are not yet "Disciples of Jesus"].

The shape of the locusts was like horses prepared for battle. On their heads were crowns of something like gold, and their faces were like the faces of men. They had hair like women's hair, and their teeth were like lions' teeth. And they had breastplates like breastplates of iron, and the sound of their wings was like the sound of chariots with many horses running into battle.

They had tails like scorpions, and there were stings in their tails. Their power was to hurt men five months [This is a five month torment—on all but the 144,000].

And they had as king over them the angel of the bottomless pit, whose name in Hebrew is Abaddon, but in Greek he has the name Apollyon.

One woe is past [The Fifth Trumpet is given the name of the "First Woe". Therefore, since one woe is past—we can understand that the "First Woe" is past. We can also understand that the time of the Fifth Trumpet is past].

Behold, still two more woes are coming after these things [The time of the "Second Woe" and the time of the "Third Woe" are coming after these things. In other words, the time of the Sixth Trumpet and the time of the Seventh Trumpet are coming after these things].

When Revelation 9:12 states, "One woe is past. Behold, still two more woes are coming after these things"—this is simply a way of letting us know that the time period of the Fifth Trumpet is definitely over and that the time period of the Sixth Trumpet and the Seventh Trumpet will follow in sequence. The time period of the Sixth Trumpet—which begins on Revelation 9:13 and ends on Revelation 11:14—may be a little longer than three and a half years—because the time of the Sixth Trumpet [the Second Woe] includes both the time of the "Seven Thunders" and the entire three and a half year time period [1,260 days] of the Ministry of the Two Prophets. Nevertheless, we can understand that Revelation 9:12 is the approximate end of the first half of the "Seven-year Tribulation" and Revelation 9:13 is the approximate beginning of the second half of the "Seven-year Tribulation".

The biblical "Sequence of Events" mentioned in Revelation concerning the first half of the "Seven-year Tribulation" is as follows.

- God takes the Scroll in His right hand. God is ready to start the final seven years and to fulfill ALL of His promises to Israel—Revelation 5:1.
- Jesus takes the Scroll from the hand of God—Revelation 5:7.
- Jesus opens the First Seal—Revelation 6:1–8.
- First Seal—one on a white horse was given a crown and he went out conquering and to conquer—Revelation 6:1–8.
- Second Seal—one on a red horse takes peace from earth—that people should kill one another—Revelation 6:1–8.
- Third Seal—one on a black horse with a pair of scales in his hand—a quart of wheat for a denarius and 3 quarts of barley for a denarius—economic hard times—Revelation 6:1–8.
- Fourth Seal—one on a pale horse whose name is Death, followed by Hades—power was given to them over a fourth of the earth—to kill with the sword, hunger, death, and by the beasts of the earth—Revelation 6:1–8.
- Suppose for example that there were a total of eight billion people living on the earth at that time. Since a fourth of the earth is killed, then that would mean that approximately two billion people will be killed during this first three and a half year period—during the first three and a half years of the "Seven-year Tribulation".
- Fifth Seal—John sees under the altar [in heaven] the souls of those who had been slain [killed] for the Word of God and for their Testimony [These are disciples of Jesus who were Faithful unto Death]—Revelation 6:9–11.
- Sixth Seal—great earthquake, the sun becomes black as sackcloth, the moon becomes like blood, stars fall, and the sky recedes like a scroll when it is rolled up, and every mountain and island is moved out of its place—Revelation 6:12–17.
- During this time, people think that this is the "Wrath of the Lamb". Nevertheless, this is NOT the "Wrath of God"; this is

- still during the first three and a half years of the "Seven-year Tribulation"—Revelation 6:12–17.
- Prior to the Seventh Seal—but still during the Sixth Seal—the 144,000 are sealed. These 144,000 are the 12,000 each from twelve tribes of Israel. These 144,000 are "hand picked" and "set apart" and "sealed"—but they are not yet "Saved"—they are not yet "Disciples of Jesus"—Revelation 7:1–17.
- Seventh Seal—there is silence in heaven for about half an hour—and the seven angels who stand before God are given Seven Trumpets—Revelation 8:1–6.
- An angel with a golden censer is given much incense and offers it with the prayers of the saints upon the altar, which is before the throne in heaven—Revelation 8:1–6.
- The angel fills the censer with fire from the altar and throws it to the earth. There are noises, thunderings, lightnings, and an earthquake—Revelation 8:1–6.
- The angels with the Seven Trumpets prepare to sound—Revelation 8:1–6.
- First Trumpet—hail and fire mingled with blood are thrown to the earth. A third of the trees are burned up and all green grass is burned up—Revelation 8:7–13.
- Second Trumpet—something like a great mountain burning with fire is thrown into the sea—a third of the sea becomes blood; a third of the creatures in the sea die; a third of all ships are destroyed—Revelation 8:7–13.
- Third Trumpet—a great star fell from heaven burning like a torch, and it fell on a third of the rivers and on the springs of water. The name of the star is Wormwood. A third of the waters became wormwood, and many men died from the water, because it was made bitter—Revelation 8:7–13.
- Fourth Trumpet—a third of the sun was struck, a third of the moon, and a third of the stars, so that a third of them were darkened. A third of the day did not shine, and likewise the night—Revelation 8:7–13.
- An angel flying through the midst of heaven says in a loud voice, "<u>Woe, Woe, Woe</u> to the inhabitants of the earth, because of the remaining blasts of the trumpet of the three angels who are about

to sound." In other words, the Fifth Trumpet is given the name "First Woe"; the Sixth Trumpet is given the name "Second Woe"; and the Seventh Trumpet is given the name "Third Woe"—Revelation 8:7–13.
- Fifth Trumpet—the bottomless pit is opened and demonic beings called locusts are given authority to harm all but the 144,000. They are given power to torment for five months. Nevertheless, they are not given authority to kill. People will seek death because of this torment, but death will flee from them—Revelation 9:1–12.
- This five month torment during the time of the Fifth Trumpet may be what Jeremiah was referring to when he spoke of "Jacob's Trouble".

> Ask now and see, whether a man is ever in labor with child? So why do I see every man with his hands on his loins like a woman in labor, and all faces turned pale? Alas! For that day is great, so that none is like it: and it is the time of "Jacob's Trouble", but he shall be saved out of it—Jeremiah 30:6–7.

- The 144,000 "shall be saved out of it"—since they are protected from the five month torment. These 144,000 are 12,000 each from twelve tribes of Israel. These 144,000 have been "hand picked" and "set apart" and "sealed"—but they are not yet "Saved"—they are not yet "Disciples of Jesus"—Revelation 7:1–17.
- Revelation 9:12 is the approximate end of the first three and a half years of the "Seven-year Tribulation".

Please understand:
My Job is NOT to convince you that the Bible is True.
My Job is to Teach you What the Bible Says.
It is the Holy Spirit's Job to convince you that the Bible is True.
Regardless of whether or not you (personally) will be alive—on the earth—during the end-time events spoken of in Revelation—it is important to understand that when Jesus told John to write to the angels of the seven churches—Jesus listed 16 Benefits of being a "Disciple of Jesus" who is "Faithful unto Death".

A "Disciple of Jesus" who is "Faithful unto Death" will:

- Be given to eat from the Tree of Life, which is in the midst of the Paradise of God—Revelation 2:7.
- Be given the Crown of Life (by Jesus)—Revelation 2:10.
- Not be hurt by the Second Death [Revelation 20:14 defines the "Second Death" as the "Lake of Fire"—therefore a "Disciple of Jesus" who is "Faithful unto Death" will not be hurt by the Lake of Fire]—Revelation 2:11.
- Be given some of the hidden manna to eat—Revelation 2:17.
- Be given a white stone (by Jesus) and on the stone will be a new name written which no one knows except him who receives it—Revelation 2:17.
- Be given power over the nations—"He shall rule them with a rod of iron: They shall be dashed to pieces like the potter's vessels"—just as Jesus received from His Father—Revelation 2:26–29.
- Be given (by Jesus) the morning star—Revelation 2:26–29.
- Be clothed in white garments—Revelation 3:5–6.
- Not have his name blotted out of the Book of Life—Revelation 3:5–6.
- Have his name confessed (by Jesus) before God and His angels—Revelation 3:5–6.
- Be made (by Jesus) to be a pillar in the Temple of God—Revelation 3:12–13.
- Be made (by Jesus) to go out no more from the Temple of God—Revelation 3:12–13.
- Have the name of God written on him (by Jesus)—Revelation 3:12–13.
- Have the name of the city of God, the New Jerusalem, which comes down out of heaven from God, written on him (by Jesus)—Revelation 3:12–13.
- Have the new name of Jesus written on him (by Jesus)—Revelation 3:12–13.
- Be granted (by Jesus) to sit with Jesus on His throne—as Jesus also overcame—and sat down with His Father on His Father's throne [Jesus was also Faithful unto Death]—Revelation 3:21–22.

Jesus instructs His disciples to "Stand" and to "Overcome" and to be "Faithful unto Death". Therefore, it is important for a disciple of Jesus to understand this Bible Truth:

> **TRIBULATION** and **PERSECUTION**
> come from our **STAND**
> on the **WORD of GOD** and our **TESTIMONY of JESUS**.

CHAPTER 5

Understanding the Final Seven Years–Part 2

Before we look at what happens during the second three and a half years of what we call the "Seven-year Tribulation"—let's look at the condition of the world at the end of the Fifth Trumpet—at the end of Revelation 9:12—at the end of the first three and a half years of the "Seven-year Tribulation".

1. The Antichrist is now firmly in power and is operating as a world leader.
2. Many disciples of Jesus were "Faithful unto Death" and were martyred for their stand on the Word of God and for their Testimony of Jesus.
3. Israel has rebuilt the Temple in Jerusalem.
4. Israel has begun observing the Daily Sacrifices at the Temple.
5. One fourth of the population of the earth has been killed during the previous three and a half years. Suppose for example that there were a total of eight billion people living on the earth when the Tribulation first began. Since one fourth of the earth has been killed, then that means that approximately two billion people have been killed during the previous three and a half years. In this example, there would now be approximately six billion people still living on the earth.
6. In addition to one fourth of the earth being killed, events in the earth and in the sky—things that are definitely not under the control of any person on the earth—have been occurring.

- Sixth Seal—there was a great earthquake, the sun became black as sackcloth, the moon became like blood, stars fell, and the sky receded like a scroll when it is rolled up. Every mountain and island were moved out of their place. During this time, people think that this is the "Wrath of the Lamb"—but this is NOT the "Wrath of God". This is still during the first three and a half years of the "Seven-year Tribulation"—Revelation 6:12–17.
- First Trumpet—hail and fire mingled with blood were thrown to the earth. A third of the trees were burned up and all green grass was burned up—Revelation 8:7–13.
- Second Trumpet—something like a great mountain burning with fire was thrown into the sea—a third of the sea became blood; a third of the creatures in the sea died; a third of all ships were destroyed—Revelation 8:7–13.
- Third Trumpet—a great star fell from heaven burning like a torch, and it fell on a third of the rivers and on the springs of water. The name of the star is Wormwood. A third of the waters became wormwood, and many died from the water, because it was made bitter—Revelation 8:7–13.
- Fourth Trumpet—a third of the sun was struck, a third of the moon, and a third of the stars, so that a third of them were darkened. A third of the day did not shine, and likewise the night—Revelation 8:7–13.
- Fifth Trumpet—the bottomless pit was opened and demonic beings called locusts were given authority to harm all but the 144,000. They were given power to torment for five months. Nevertheless, they were not given authority to kill. People sought death because of this torment, but they were unable to die—Revelation 9:1–12.
- This five month torment during the time of the Fifth Trumpet may be what Jeremiah was referring to when he spoke of "Jacob's Trouble".

> Ask now and see, whether a man is ever in labor with child? So why do I see every man with his hands on his loins like a woman in labor, and all faces turned

pale? Alas! For that day is great, so that none is like it: and it is the time of "Jacob's Trouble", but he shall be saved out of it—Jeremiah 30:6–7.

- The 144,000 were saved out of it—since they were protected from the five month torment. These 144,000 are 12,000 each from twelve tribes of Israel. These 144,000 have been "hand picked" and "set apart" and "sealed"—but they are not yet "Saved"—they are not yet "Disciples of Jesus"—Revelation 7:1–17.

God has promised both in the Old Testament Scriptures and in the New Testament Scriptures that "Israel will be saved". Nevertheless, Israel must be "saved" the same way any person is "saved". Paul taught that an individual is saved by grace through faith. Consider Ephesians 2:8–9: "For by grace you have been saved through faith, and that not of yourselves; it is the gift of God, not of works, lest anyone should boast."

In Romans 10:8–13, Paul taught the following.

But what does it [the Scripture] say? "The word is near you, in your mouth and in your heart" (that is, the word of faith which we preach): that if you confess with your mouth the Lord Jesus and believe in your heart that God has raised Him from the dead, you will be saved. For with the heart one believes unto righteousness, and with the mouth confession is made unto salvation. For the Scripture says, "Whoever believes on Him will not be put to shame." For there is no distinction between Jew and Greek [the 144,000 must be "Saved" the same way that anyone is "Saved"], for the same Lord over all is rich to all who call upon Him. For "whoever calls on the name of the Lord shall be saved."

Revelation 9:12 is the approximate end of the first half of the "Seven-year Tribulation". Revelation 9:13 is the approximate beginning of the second half of the "Seven-year Tribulation".

Then during the Sixth Trumpet—during the second three and a half years of the "Seven-year Tribulation", God will send the two witnesses—His Two Prophets discussed in Revelation 11:1–14—and they will teach "Jesus is the Messiah" to the 144,000—from the Temple in Jerusalem—for three and a half years.

During their 1,260-day (three and a half year) ministry, every single one of the 144,000 will be saved—12,000 each from the twelve tribes of Israel will be saved—and every single one will become a disciple of Jesus. In fact, every single one of these 144,000 will be "Faithful unto Death" and we will see them in heaven—during the Seventh Trumpet—<u>prior to the Rapture</u>—and they are described as "ones who follow the Lamb wherever He goes" (Revelation 14:1–5).

Therefore, Israel will be saved—and God's promise to save Israel will be fulfilled—and all of this will occur <u>prior to the Rapture</u>—prior to the end of the Seventh Trumpet.

In the previous chapter we saw what happened during the first half of what we call the "Seven-year Tribulation". In this chapter we will look at what happens during the second half of the "Seven-year Tribulation"—during the time of the Sixth Trumpet.

In Revelation 9:13, the Sixth Trumpet sounds.

> Then the sixth angel sounded [The Sixth Trumpet is given the name of the "Second Woe"]: And I heard a voice from the four horns of the golden altar which is before God, saying to the sixth angel who had the trumpet, "Release the four angels who are bound at the great river Euphrates."
>
> So the four angels, who had been prepared for the hour and day and month and year, were released to kill a third of mankind.
>
> Now the number of the army of the horsemen was two hundred million; I heard the number of them. And thus I saw the horses in the vision: those who sat on them had breastplates of fiery red, hyacinth blue, and sulfur yellow; and the heads of the horses were like the heads of lions; and out of their mouths came fire, smoke, and brimstone.

By these three plagues a third of mankind was killed—by the fire and the smoke and the brimstone which came out of their mouths. For their power is in their mouth and in their tails; for their tails are like serpents, having heads; and with them they do harm.

But the rest of mankind, who were not killed by these plagues, did not repent of the works of their hands, that they should not worship demons, and idols of gold, silver, brass, stone, and wood, which can neither see nor hear nor walk.

And they did not repent of their murders or their sorceries [some versions of the Bible translate the word used for "sorceries" as "drugs"] or their sexual immorality or their thefts.

In Revelation 10:1–11, John heard the "Seven Thunders"—but was told not to write what the "Seven Thunders" had uttered.

I saw still another mighty angel coming down from heaven, clothed with a cloud. And a rainbow was on his head, his face was like the sun, and his feet like pillars of fire. He had a little book open in his hand. And he set his right foot on the sea and his left foot on the land, and cried with a loud voice, as when a lion roars. When he cried out, seven thunders [Seven Thunders] uttered their voices.

Now when the seven thunders [Seven Thunders] uttered their voices, I was about to write; but I heard a voice from heaven saying to me, "Seal up the things which the seven thunders uttered, and do not write them."

The angel whom I saw standing on the sea and on the land raised up his hand to heaven and swore by Him who lives forever and ever, who created heaven and the things that are in it, the earth and the things that are in it, and the sea and the things that are in it, that there should be delay no longer, but in the days of the sounding of the seventh angel [the Seventh Trumpet], when he is about to sound, the mystery of God would be finished, as He declared to His servants the prophets.

Then the voice which I heard from heaven spoke to me again and said, "Go, take the little book which is open in the hand of the angel who stands on the sea and on the earth."

So I went to the angel and said to him, "Give me the little book."

And he said to me, "Take and eat it; and it will make your stomach bitter, but it will be as sweet as honey in your mouth."

Then I took the little book out of the angel's hand and ate it, and it was as sweet as honey in my mouth. But when I had eaten it, my stomach became bitter.

And he said to me, "You must prophesy again about many peoples, nations, tongues, and kings."

In Revelation 11:1–14, the Temple and the 1,260-day ministry of the two witnesses [the Two Prophets] are discussed.

> Then I was given a reed like a measuring rod. And the angel stood, saying, "Rise and measure the temple of God [the Temple in Jerusalem], the altar, and those who worship there.
>
> But leave out the court which is outside the temple, and do not measure it, for it has been given to the Gentiles.

And they will tread the holy city [Jerusalem] underfoot for forty-two months [three and a half years].

And I will give power to my two witnesses [the Two Prophets], and they will prophesy one thousand two hundred and sixty days [the same three and a half years], clothed in sackcloth."

These are the two olive trees and the two lampstands standing before the God of the earth.

And if anyone wants to harm them [the Two Prophets], fire proceeds from their mouth and devours their enemies. And if anyone wants to harm them [the Two Prophets], he must be killed in this manner.

These [the Two Prophets] have power to shut heaven, so that no rain falls in the days of their prophecy; and they have power over waters to turn them to blood, and to strike the earth with all plagues, as often as they desire.

When they finish their testimony, the beast that ascends out of the bottomless pit [Satan] will make war against them, overcome them, and kill them.

And their dead bodies will lie in the street of the great city which spiritually is called Sodom and Egypt, where also our Lord was crucified [Jerusalem].

Then those from the peoples, tribes, tongues, and nations will see their dead bodies three-and-a-half days, and not allow their dead bodies to be put into graves. And those who dwell on the earth will rejoice over them, make merry, and send gifts to one another, because these two prophets [the Two Prophets] tormented those who dwell on the earth.

Now after the three-and-a-half days the breath of life from God entered them, and they [the Two Prophets] stood on their feet, and great fear fell on those who saw them.

And they heard a loud voice from heaven saying to them, "Come up here." And they ascended to heaven in a cloud, and their enemies saw them.

In the same hour there was a great earthquake, and a tenth of the city [Jerusalem] fell. In the earthquake seven thousand people were killed, and the rest were afraid and gave glory to the God of heaven.

The second woe is past [The Sixth Trumpet is given the name of the "Second Woe". Therefore, since the "Second Woe" is past—we can understand that the Sixth Trumpet is past].

Behold, the third woe is coming quickly [The Seventh Trumpet is given the name of the "Third Woe". Therefore, since the "Third Woe" is coming quickly—we can understand that the Seventh Trumpet is coming quickly].

When Revelation 11:14 states, "The second woe is past. Behold, the third woe is coming quickly"—this is simply a way of letting us know that the time of the Sixth Trumpet is definitely over and that the time period of the Seventh Trumpet is coming quickly.

The Seventh Trumpet (the "Third Woe") includes information about the "Summary of Revelation 12:1–14:20", information about an "Angel Preaching the Gospel to those on the earth prior to the Rapture", information about two other Angels proclaiming their messages to those on the earth prior to the Rapture, and information about the Rapture—which will occur at the end of the time period of the Seventh Trumpet.

But why is the time of the Seventh Trumpet also called the "Third Woe"?

In Revelation 11:7—during the time of the Sixth Trumpet—the Two Prophets were killed. This occurred on approximately the 1,260th day of their three and a half year ministry. Therefore, several days after Revelation 11:7—on the 1,290th day—one thousand two hundred and ninety days after the Antichrist stopped the "Daily Sacrifices" at the Temple—the Antichrist will commit the "Abomination of Desolation" [which occurs inside the Temple]. This will begin the approximately 45-day time period that Jesus referred to as the "Great Tribulation"—where Jesus said that it had never been that bad before and that it would never be that bad again (Mathew 24:15–22).

The time of the "Third Woe" will also be the time when the "False Prophet" will issue a decree that anyone not taking the "Mark of the Beast" [the Mark of the Antichrist] will be killed, thus creating a time where <u>it has never been that bad before</u> and where <u>it will never be that bad again.</u>

One fourth of the earth was killed during the first three and a half years of the "Seven-year Tribulation" (Revelation 5:1–9:12). Another one third of the earth was killed during the second three and a half years of the "Seven-year Tribulation"—during the Sixth Trumpet—during the time period of Revelation 9:13–11:14. As bad as all of that was—this 45-day time period of the "Third Woe"—this 45-day time period of the Seventh Trumpet—this 45-day time period of Revelation 11:15–14:20—this 45-day time period which begins when the Antichrist commits the "Abomination of Desolation"—this 45-day time period referred to by Jesus as the "Great Tribulation"—will be worse! It will be a time where <u>it has never been that bad before</u> and it will be a time where <u>it will never be that bad again</u>.

Suppose for example that there were a total of eight billion people living on the earth when the Tribulation first began. Since one fourth of the earth will be killed during the first half of the "Seven-year Tribulation", then that would mean that approximately two billion people will be killed during that time. In this example, there would now be approximately six billion people still living on the earth when the Sixth Trumpet sounded. Since another one third of the earth will be killed during the time period of the Sixth Trumpet, then that would mean that another approximately two billion people will be killed during the second half of the "Seven-year Tribulation". In this example, that would mean that four billion people would have been killed during the entire time period of the "Seven-year

Tribulation" and there would now be approximately four billion people still living on the earth when the Seventh Trumpet sounded.

These four billion people will be faced with the decision of whether or not to take the "Mark of the Beast" [the Mark of the Antichrist]—knowing that if they do not take the "Mark of the Beast"—they will be killed. This is the time that Jesus referred to as the "Great Tribulation" and this is what Revelation refers to as the "Third Woe". This period will only last approximately 45 days. Nevertheless, this will be a time where <u>it has never been that bad before</u> and this will be a time where <u>it will never be that bad again</u>.

Nevertheless, during this same time period an Angel will be Preaching the Gospel to those on the earth, and a second Angel will be saying, "Babylon is fallen, is fallen", and a third Angel will be warning people to NOT take the "Mark of the Beast". All of this will take place during the time period of the Seventh Trumpet—during the time period of the "Great Tribulation"—and <u>prior to the Rapture</u>.

By this time in history, Babylon will have become a great city (again). Just as it was tough for many people [prior to 1948] to understand that Israel would become a nation (again) and that Israel would one day rebuild the Temple (again)—it will also be tough for many people to understand that Babylon will one day become a great city (again)—even though the Bible has prophesied that Babylon will be "that great city Babylon, that mighty city!" (Revelation 18:10).

Here is a quick summary of events.

1. The first three and a half years of the "Seven-year Tribulation".

   - The Seven Seals.
   - The First Four Trumpets.
   - The Fifth Trumpet (the First Woe).

2. The second three and a half years of the "Seven-year Tribulation".

   - The Sixth Trumpet (the Second Woe).

3. The Seventh Trumpet (the Third Woe) is approximately a 45-day period of time, but several major events take place during the time period of the Seventh Trumpet.

- Abomination of Desolation [which occurs inside the Temple]. This event occurs approximately 1,290 days after the Antichrist stopped the "Daily Sacrifices" at the Temple in Jerusalem. This event occurs after the Two Prophets have been killed.
- The decree by the "False Prophet" that every single person living on the earth will be required to take the "Mark of the Antichrist" or be killed.
- The "Great Tribulation"—the time period that Jesus referred to where it has never been that bad before and where it will never be that bad again.
- The "Summary of Revelation 12:1–14:20".
- An Angel Preaches the Gospel to those on the earth prior to the Rapture. (Revelation 14:6–7)
- A second Angel follows and says, "Babylon is fallen, is fallen, that great city, because she has made all nations drink of the wine of the wrath of her fornication." (Revelation 14:8)
- A third Angel followed them, saying with a loud voice, "If anyone worships the beast [the Antichrist], and receives his mark on his forehead or on his hand [the Mark of the Antichrist], he himself shall also drink of the wine of the Wrath of God [the Wrath of God] which is poured out full strength into the cup of His indignation. He shall be tormented with fire and brimstone in the presence of the holy angels and in the presence of the Lamb [Jesus]. And the smoke of their torment ascends forever and ever; and they shall have no rest day or night, who worship the beast [the Antichrist] and his image [the image of the Antichrist], and whoever receives the mark of his name [whoever receives the Mark of the Antichrist]. (Revelation 14:9–11)
- The Rapture. This event occurs after these three Angels have proclaimed their messages to the people on the earth. This event occurs approximately 1,335 days after the Antichrist has stopped the "Daily Sacrifices" at the Temple in Jerusalem. In other words, this event occurs approximately 45 days after the Antichrist has committed the "Abomination of Desolation" [which occurs inside the Temple].

4. The Wrath of God. The Wrath of God is approximately a 965-day period of time—almost three years—where the Seven Bowls of the "Wrath of God" are poured out onto an unsaved world—upon the whole world—to test those who dwell on the earth. The destruction of Babylon and the Battle of Armageddon both occur during the time period of the Wrath of God. After the Battle of Armageddon is over, the Antichrist and the False Prophet are cast alive into the Lake of Fire—and Satan is bound and thrown into a bottomless pit for 1,000 years. This ends the time period of the Wrath of God. (Revelation 15:1–19:21)
5. Jesus rules on the earth from Jerusalem for 1,000 years—while Satan is locked up in the bottomless pit during the same 1,000-year period. At the end of the 1,000 years—when Satan is released—Satan gathers an army to attack Jerusalem and to fight Jesus. Satan is overthrown by God and is cast into the Lake of Fire—where the Antichrist and the False Prophet are. (Revelation 20:1–10)
6. The "Great White Throne" Judgment. The Book of Life is opened and those whose names are not found written in the Book of Life are cast into the Lake of Fire. (Revelation 20:11–15)
7. There is a "New Heaven" and a "New Earth". (Revelation 21:1–22:21)

In the next chapter, we will look at the Seventh Trumpet (the Third Woe) and the "Summary of Revelation 12:1–14:20".

As strange as it may sound, God may choose to show this "Summary of Revelation 12:1–14:20" to the people who are still alive on the earth during the time of the Seventh Trumpet—perhaps something like a "Drive-in Movie in the Sky"—or perhaps something like a vision that everyone sees—or perhaps something similar to the way that God showed this same "Summary" to John. John writes, "Now a great sign appeared in heaven..." (Revelation 12:1–14:20)

Of course, God may not choose to do that—and in that case—the "Summary of Revelation 12:1–14:20" would simply be for our benefit—for those of us who read and understand the "Summary of Revelation 12:1–14:20". This case is also very possible—because the "Summary" provides us with at least two pieces of "New Information" that we do not find anywhere else in the Bible. In addition, the "Summary" also confirms the Biblical "Sequence of Events" that we have seen throughout the Old Testament and the New Testament Scriptures.

- Tribulation
- Rapture
- Wrath of God

We will look at both cases in the next chapter.

CHAPTER 6

Understanding the Seventh Trumpet and the Summary of Revelation 12:1–14:20

As mentioned earlier, the Seventh Trumpet—also known as the "Third Woe"—is approximately a 45-day period of time. The "Abomination of Desolation" can not occur during the time of the 1,260 day Ministry of the Two Prophets—because of the tremendous power given to the Two Prophets—but it does occur shortly after the Two Prophets have been killed. Therefore, the time period of the Seventh Trumpet (the Third Woe) includes each of the following major events.

- Abomination of Desolation [which occurs inside the Temple]. This event occurs approximately 1,290 days after the Antichrist stopped the "Daily Sacrifices" at the Temple in Jerusalem. This event occurs after the Two Prophets have been killed.
- The decree by the "False Prophet" that every single person living on the earth will be required to take the "Mark of the Antichrist" or be killed.
- The "Great Tribulation"—the time period that Jesus referred to where it has never been that bad before and where it will never be that bad again.
- The "Summary of Revelation 12:1–14:20".
- An Angel Preaches the Gospel to those on the earth prior to the Rapture. (Revelation 14:6–7)
- A second Angel follows and says, "Babylon is fallen, is fallen, that great city, because she has made all nations drink of the wine of the wrath of her fornication. (Revelation 14:8)

- A third Angel followed them, saying with a loud voice, "If anyone worships the beast [the Antichrist], and receives his mark on his forehead or on his hand [the Mark of the Antichrist], he himself shall also drink of the wine of the Wrath of God [the Wrath of God] which is poured out full strength into the cup of His indignation. He shall be tormented with fire and brimstone in the presence of the holy angels and in the presence of the Lamb [Jesus]. And the smoke of their torment ascends forever and ever; and they shall have no rest day or night, who worship the beast [the Antichrist] and his image [the image of the Antichrist], and whoever receives the mark of his name [whoever receives the Mark of the Antichrist]. (Revelation 14:9–11)
- The Rapture. This event occurs after these three Angels have proclaimed their messages to the people on the earth. This event occurs approximately 1,335 days after the Antichrist has stopped the "Daily Sacrifices" at the Temple in Jerusalem. In other words, this event occurs approximately 45 days after the Antichrist has committed the "Abomination of Desolation" [which occurs inside the Temple].

Let's look at what Revelation says about the Seventh Trumpet and about the "Summary of Revelation 12:1–14:20".

In Revelation 11:15–19, the Seventh Angel sounds.

> Then the seventh angel sounded [The Seventh Trumpet is given the name of the "Third Woe"]: And there were loud voices in heaven, saying, "The kingdoms of this world have become the kingdoms of our Lord and of His Christ, and He shall reign forever and ever!"

> And the twenty-four elders who sat before God on their thrones fell on their faces and worshiped God, saying: "We give You thanks, O Lord God Almighty, The One who is and who was and who is to come, Because You have taken Your great power and reigned.

> The nations were angry, and Your wrath has come,
> And the time of the dead, that they should be judged,
> And that You should reward Your servants the prophets and the saints,
> And those who fear Your name, small and great,
> And should destroy those who destroy the earth."
> Then the temple of God was opened in heaven, and the ark of His covenant was seen in His temple.
> And there were lightnings, noises, thunderings, an earthquake, and great hail.

In Revelation 12:1–14:20, during the time period of the Seventh Trumpet (the "Third Woe"), John is shown the "Summary of Revelation 12:1–14:20". As mentioned earlier—as strange as it may sound—God may choose to show this "Summary" to the people who are still alive on the earth during the time of the Seventh Trumpet—perhaps something like a "Drive-in Movie in the Sky"—or perhaps something like a vision that everyone sees—or perhaps something similar to the way that God showed this same "Summary" to John. Let's look at this case first.

> Now a great sign appeared in heaven: a woman clothed with the sun [This appears to be a reference to the nation of Israel], with the moon under her feet, and on her head a garland of twelve stars [This appears to be a reference to the twelve sons of Israel—the twelve Tribes of Israel].
>
> Then being with child, she cried out in labor and in pain to give birth [This appears to be a reference to the nation of Israel ready to give birth to the Messiah—Jesus].
>
> And another sign appeared in heaven: behold, a great, fiery red dragon having seven heads and ten horns, and seven diadems on his heads [This appears to be a reference to Satan].
>
> His tail drew a third of the stars of heaven and threw them to the earth [This is NOT the "War in Heaven"—instead,

this appears to be a reference to the fact that Satan was able to somehow convince one third of the angels to follow him and to rebel against God and to turn their backs on God. These demonic angels choose to follow Satan—and are drawn to the earth—by Satan—to kill, steal, and destroy on the earth].

And the dragon [Satan] stood before the woman [Israel] who was ready to give birth [Israel was ready to give birth to the Messiah—Jesus], to devour her Child [to devour the Messiah—Jesus] as soon as it was born.

She [Israel] bore a male Child [the Messiah—Jesus] who was to rule all nations with a rod of iron [Jesus will rule the world—from Jerusalem—for 1,000 years].

And her Child [the Messiah—Jesus] was caught up to God and His throne [The Messiah—Jesus—ascended to Heaven—after He had done the work necessary to bring in the New Covenant—which is available to both you and me—through His work on the Cross. Jesus now sits at the right hand of the Throne of God].

Then the woman [Israel] fled into the wilderness [This appears to be a reference to the Temple—where Israel will be ministered to by the Two Prophets for 1,260 days], where she [Israel] has a place prepared by God [the Temple in Jerusalem], that they [the Two Prophets] should feed her there one thousand two hundred and sixty days [The Two Prophets will feed Israel—both physically and spiritually—from the Temple—in Jerusalem—for 1,260 days—three and a half years—during the time of the Sixth Trumpet. These Two Prophets will teach "Jesus is the Messiah" to the 144,000—and to all others who will come to the Temple to hear the Word of God—during that three and a half year period].

And war broke out in heaven: Michael and his angels fought with the dragon; and the dragon and his angels fought, but they did not prevail, nor was a place found for them in heaven any longer [Michael and the holy angels fight in this "War in Heaven" with Satan and the demonic angels. Satan loses that fight. Satan and the demonic angels are kicked out of Heaven. They are cast to the earth and are no longer given access to Heaven].

So the great dragon was cast out, that serpent of old, called the Devil and Satan, who deceives the whole world; he was cast to the earth, and his angels were cast out with him [Satan and the demonic angels are kicked out of Heaven. They are cast to the earth and are no longer given access to Heaven].

Then I heard a loud voice saying in heaven, "Now salvation, and strength, and the kingdom of our God, and the power of His Christ have come, for the accuser of our brethren, who accused them before our God day and night, has been cast down [Satan and the demonic angels are kicked out of Heaven. They are cast to the earth and are no longer given access to Heaven].

And they overcame him [Satan] by the <u>Blood of the Lamb</u> and by the <u>Word of their Testimony</u>, and <u>they did not love their lives to the death</u> [Faithful unto Death].

Therefore rejoice, O heavens, and you who dwell in them!

Woe to the inhabitants of the earth and the sea! For the devil has come down to you, having great wrath, because he knows that he has a short time [Satan and the demonic angels are kicked out of Heaven. They are cast to the earth and are no longer given access to Heaven].

Now when the dragon [Satan] saw that he had been cast to the earth, he persecuted the woman [Israel] who gave birth to the male Child [Jesus].

But the woman [Israel] was given two wings of a great eagle [This appears to be a reference to the protection and the provision of the Two Prophets], that she [Israel] might fly into the wilderness to her place [the Temple in Jerusalem], where she [Israel] is nourished [Israel is fed both physically and spiritually by the Two Prophets] for a time and times and half a time [three and a half years], from the presence of the serpent [The Two Prophets will protect Israel from Satan and his demonic angels. The Two Prophets will also feed Israel—both physically and spiritually—from the Temple—in Jerusalem—for 1,260 days. The Two Prophets will teach "Jesus is the Messiah" to the 144,000—and to all others who will come to the Temple to hear the Word of God—for three and a half years—during the time period of the Sixth Trumpet].

So the serpent [Satan] spewed water out of his mouth like a flood after the woman [Israel], that he might cause her [Israel] to be carried away by the flood.

But the earth helped the woman [Israel], and the earth opened its mouth and swallowed up the flood which the dragon [Satan] had spewed out of his mouth.

And the dragon [Satan] was enraged with the woman [Israel], and he [Satan] went to make war with the rest of her offspring, who keep the commandments of God and have the Testimony of Jesus Christ [Satan is enraged because he is prevented by the Two Prophets from harming Israel—so Satan goes to make war with the rest of her offspring—Christians—Disciples of Jesus—who keep the commandments of God and have the Testimony of Jesus Christ].

Then I stood on the sand of the sea. And I saw a beast rising up out of the sea, having seven heads and ten horns, and on his horns ten crowns, and on his heads a blasphemous name [This appears to be a reference to the Antichrist].

Now the beast [the Antichrist] which I saw was like a leopard, his feet were like the feet of a bear, and his mouth like the mouth of a lion. The dragon [Satan] gave him [the Antichrist] his power, his throne, and great authority. And I saw one of his heads as if it had been mortally wounded, and his deadly wound was healed. And all the world marveled and followed the beast [All the world followed the Antichrist].

So they worshiped the dragon [Satan] who gave authority to the beast [the Antichrist]; and they worshiped the beast [the Antichrist], saying, "Who is like the beast [the Antichrist]? Who is able to make war with him?"

And he [the Antichrist] was given a mouth speaking great things and blasphemies, and he [the Antichrist] was given authority to continue for forty-two months [three and a half years].

Then he [the Antichrist] opened his mouth in blasphemy against God, to blaspheme His name, His tabernacle, and those who dwell in heaven.

It was granted to him [the Antichrist] to make war with the saints [Christians—Disciples of Jesus] and to overcome them [kill them].

And authority was given him [the Antichrist] over every tribe, tongue, and nation.

All who dwell on the earth will worship him [the Antichrist], whose names have not been written in the Book of Life of the Lamb slain from the foundation of the world.

If anyone has an ear, let him hear [Understand].

He who leads into captivity shall go into captivity; he who kills with the sword must be killed with the sword. Here is the patience and the faith of the saints.

Then I saw another beast [the False Prophet] coming up out of the earth, and he [the False Prophet] had two horns like a lamb and spoke like a dragon.

And he [the False Prophet] exercises all the authority of the first beast [the Antichrist] in his presence, and causes the earth and those who dwell in it to worship the first beast [the Antichrist], whose deadly wound was healed [The False Prophet causes those on earth to worship the Antichrist].

He [the False Prophet] performs great signs, so that he [the False Prophet] even makes fire come down from heaven on the earth in the sight of men.

And he [the False Prophet] deceives those who dwell on the earth by those signs which he was granted to do in the sight of the beast [in the sight of the Antichrist], telling those who dwell on the earth to make an image to the beast [the Antichrist] who was wounded by the sword and lived.

He [the False Prophet] was granted power to give breath to the image of the beast [the image of the Antichrist], that the image of the beast [the image of the Antichrist] should both speak and cause as many as would not worship the image of the beast to be killed [all those who would not worship the image of the Antichrist were killed].

He [the False Prophet] causes all, both small and great, rich and poor, free and slave, to receive a mark on their right hand or on their foreheads [This is the Mark of the Antichrist], and that no one may buy or sell except one who has the mark or the name of the beast, or the number of his name [Only those who have the Mark of the Antichrist, or the name of the Antichrist, or the number of the Antichrist are allowed to buy or sell].

Here is wisdom. Let him who has understanding calculate the number of the beast [the number of the Antichrist], for it is the number of a man: His number is 666.

Then I looked, and behold, a Lamb [Jesus] standing on Mount Zion [this is the Mount Zion in Heaven—as described in Hebrews 12:22–24], and with Him [Jesus] one hundred and forty-four thousand, having His Father's name written on their foreheads. [These are the 144,000 who were "selected" and "set apart" and "sealed"—but who were not yet "Saved"—when the Sixth Trumpet first began. Now—after the three and a half year Ministry of the Two Prophets—we see that they are all "Saved" and in Heaven with Jesus. Since this is still prior to the Rapture—we can understand that each one of the 144,000—each one of 12,000 each from the Twelve Tribes of Israel—were all "Faithful unto Death". Most Bible references to Mount Zion refer to the Mount Zion in Israel. Nevertheless, Hebrews 12:22–24 tells us about the Mount Zion discussed here—the Mount Zion in heaven. "But you have come to Mount Zion and to the city of the living God, the heavenly Jerusalem, to an innumerable company of angels, to the general assembly and church of the firstborn who are registered in heaven, to God the judge of all, to the spirits of just men made perfect, to Jesus the Mediator of the new covenant, and to the sprinkling that speaks better things than that of Abel."]

And I heard a voice from heaven, like the voice of many waters, and like the voice of loud thunder. And I heard the sound of harpists playing their harps.

They [the 144,000—who are now "Saved" and in Heaven] sang as it were a new song before the throne, before the four living creatures, and the elders; and no one could learn that song except the hundred and forty-four thousand who were redeemed from the earth [This is clearly the Throne of God—in Heaven].

These [the 144,000—who are now "Saved" and in Heaven] are the ones who were not defiled with women, for they are virgins.

These [the 144,000—who are now "Saved" and in Heaven] are the ones who follow the Lamb [Jesus] wherever He goes [The 144,000 are disciples of Jesus].

These [the 144,000—who are now "Saved" and in Heaven] were redeemed from among men, being firstfruits to God and to the Lamb [Jesus].

And in their mouth was found no deceit, for they [the 144,000—who are now "Saved" and in Heaven] are without fault before the Throne of God.

Then I saw another angel flying in the midst of heaven, having the everlasting gospel to preach to those who dwell on the earth—to every nation, tribe, tongue, and people—saying with a loud voice, "Fear God and give glory to Him, for the hour of His judgment has come; and worship Him who made heaven and earth, the sea and springs of water" [This event—the message of the First

Angel—takes place during the "Great Tribulation"—during the time period of the Seventh Trumpet (the Third Woe)—and prior to the Rapture. The strong implication here is that a person can still be "Saved"].

And another angel followed, saying, "Babylon is fallen, is fallen, that great city, because she has made all nations drink of the wine of the wrath of her fornication" [This event—the message of the Second Angel—takes place during the "Great Tribulation—during the time period of the Seventh Trumpet (the Third Woe)—and prior to the Rapture. As mentioned earlier—at this point in history—Babylon is a great city. The destruction of Babylon is prophesied throughout the Bible].

Then a third angel followed them, saying with a loud voice, "If anyone worships the beast [the Antichrist] and his image [the image of the Antichrist], and receives his mark [the Mark of the Antichrist] on his forehead or on his hand, he himself shall also drink of the wine of the Wrath of God [the Wrath of God], which is poured out full strength into the cup of His indignation.

He [the person who takes the Mark of the Antichrist] shall be tormented with fire and brimstone in the presence of the holy angels and in the presence of the Lamb [Jesus]. And the smoke of their torment ascends forever and ever; and they have no rest day or night, who worship the beast [the Antichrist] and his image [the image of the Antichrist], and whoever receives the mark of his name [the Mark of the Antichrist]." [This event—the message of the Third Angel—takes place during the "Great Tribulation"—during the time period of the Seventh Trumpet (the Third Woe)—and prior to the Rapture.]

Here is the patience of the saints [Christians—Disciples of Jesus]; here are those who keep the commandments of God and the faith of Jesus.

Then I heard a voice from heaven saying to me, "Write: 'Blessed are the dead who die in the Lord from now on.'"

"Yes," says the Spirit, "that they may rest from their labors, and their works follow them."

Then I looked, and behold, a white cloud, and on the cloud sat One like the Son of Man [Jesus], having on His head a golden crown, and in His hand a sharp sickle.

And another angel came out of the temple, crying with a loud voice to Him [Jesus] who sat on the cloud, "Thrust in Your sickle and reap, for the time has come for You to reap, for the harvest of the earth is ripe."

So He [Jesus] who sat on the cloud thrust in His sickle on the earth, and the earth was reaped [This is a "picture" of the "Rapture"].

Then another angel came out of the temple which is in heaven, he also having a sharp sickle. And another angel came out from the altar, who had power over fire, and he cried with a loud cry to him who had the sharp sickle, saying, "Thrust in your sharp sickle and gather the clusters of the vine of the earth, for her grapes are fully ripe."

So the angel thrust his sickle into the earth and gathered the vine of the earth, and threw it into the great winepress of the Wrath of God [This is a "picture" of the "Wrath of God"].

And the winepress was trampled outside the city, and blood came out of the winepress, up to the horses' bridles, for one thousand six hundred furlongs [This appears to be is a reference to the Battle of Armageddon—which occurs during the time period of the Seventh Bowl of the "Wrath of God." The Battle of Armageddon results in blood up to the horses' bridles for approximately 160-plus miles].

As mentioned earlier—as strange as it may sound—God may choose to show the "Summary of Revelation 12:1–14:20"—which we have just looked at—to the people who are still alive on the earth during the time of the Seventh Trumpet—perhaps something like a "Drive-in Movie in the Sky"—or perhaps something like a vision that everyone sees—or perhaps something similar to the way that God showed this same "Summary" to John. If that is the case, then as soon as this "Summary" is over—the Rapture will occur.

Once the Rapture occurs—the only ones still on the earth will be people who are not saved and demons. Then the Seven Bowls of the "Wrath of God" will be poured out onto an unsaved world—upon the whole world—to test those who dwell on the earth.

If God does not choose to show this "Summary" to the people on the earth who are still alive during the time of the Seventh Trumpet (the Third Woe)—and that case is also very possible—then we can still learn some important information from reading and understanding this "Summary".

First of all, the Biblical "Sequence of Events" given in the "Summary" lines up with what we have seen throughout the Bible—so the "Summary" actually confirms the Biblical "Sequence of Events":

- Tribulation
- Rapture
- Wrath of God

Secondly, there are at least two pieces of "New Information" that we only find here in the "Summary":

- The "Summary" shows us information that the 144,000 are definitely "Saved"—<u>prior to the Rapture</u>.

- The "Summary" shows us information that an Angel preaches the Gospel to those on the earth—prior to the Rapture.

Regardless of whether or not God chooses to show this "Summary" to those still living on the earth during the time period of the Seventh Trumpet (the Third Woe)—the three Angels will still definitely fly in the midst of heaven and proclaim their messages to those who dwell on the earth—to every nation, tribe, tongue, and people—and this will definitely happen prior to the Rapture.

Therefore, even if God does not choose to show this "Summary" to those people who are still alive on the earth during the time of the Seventh Trumpet (the Third Woe)—during the time period of the "Great Tribulation"—during the time where it has never been that bad before and where it will never be that bad again—even in that case—the event concerning the messages of the three Angels (which is recorded in Revelation 14:6–11) will still occur—prior to the Rapture.

> Then I saw another angel flying in the midst of heaven, having the everlasting gospel to preach to those who dwell on the earth—to every nation, tribe, tongue, and people—saying with a loud voice, "Fear God and give glory to Him, for the hour of His judgment has come; and worship Him who made heaven and earth, the sea and springs of water."
>
> And another angel followed, saying, "Babylon is fallen, is fallen, that great city, because she has made all nations drink of the wine of the wrath of her fornication."
>
> Then a third angel followed them, saying with a loud voice, "If anyone worships the beast and his image, and receives his mark on his forehead or on his hand, he himself shall also drink of the wine of the Wrath of God, which is poured out full strength into the cup of His indignation.
>
> He shall be tormented with fire and brimstone in the presence of the holy angels and in the presence of the

Lamb. And the smoke of their torment ascends forever and ever; and they have no rest day or night, who worship the beast and his image, and whoever receives the mark of his name."

Once these three Angels have proclaimed their messages to the entire world—the Rapture will occur. Once the Rapture occurs—the following major events will occur.

- The Wrath of God.
- The 1,000 year reign of Jesus—who will rule the world from Jerusalem.
- The "Great White Throne" Judgment.
- The "New Heaven" and the "New Earth".

We will look at the Seven Bowls of the "Wrath of God"—and these three other major events—in the next chapter.

CHAPTER 7

Understanding the Seven Bowls of the Wrath of God

As we begin this chapter, the Rapture has just occurred, all Christians are in heaven with Jesus, and God is ready to pour out the Seven Bowls of the "Wrath of God" onto an unsaved world—upon the whole world—to test those who dwell on the earth. Nevertheless, we never read in Scripture of anyone getting saved after the Rapture. Instead, we are repeatedly told, "They would not repent" and "They blasphemed God."

Throughout the first six chapters of this book, I have used the New King James Version. In this chapter, I will use the King James Version. We will look at the following four major events.

- The Seven Bowls of the "Wrath of God".
- The 1,000 year reign of Jesus—who will rule the world from Jerusalem.
- The "Great White Throne" Judgment.
- The "New Heaven" and the "New Earth".

In Revelation 15:1–8 (KJV), John is shown the Seven Angels who have the Seven Bowls of the "Wrath of God".

> And I saw another sign in heaven, great and marvellous, seven angels having the seven last plagues [the Seven Bowls of the "Wrath of God"]; for in them is filled up the Wrath of God.

And I saw as it were a sea of glass mingled with fire: and them that had gotten the victory over the beast, and over his image, and over his mark, and over the number of his name, stand on the sea of glass, having the harps of God [These are the "Disciples of Jesus" who were "Faithful unto Death"].

And they sing the song of Moses the servant of God, and the song of the Lamb, saying, Great and marvellous are thy works, Lord God Almighty; just and true are thy ways, thou King of saints.

Who shall not fear thee, O Lord, and glorify thy name? for thou only art holy: for all nations shall come and worship before thee; for thy judgments are made manifest.

And after that I looked, and, behold, the temple of the tabernacle of the testimony in heaven was opened:

And the seven angels came out of the temple, having the seven plagues [the Seven Bowls of the "Wrath of God"], clothed in pure and white linen, and having their breasts girded with golden girdles.

And one of the four beasts gave unto the seven angels seven golden vials full of the Wrath of God, who liveth for ever and ever.

And the temple was filled with smoke from the glory of God, and from his power; and no man was able to enter into the temple, till the seven plagues of the seven angels were fulfilled [No one was able to enter the Temple in Heaven until the Seven Bowls of the "Wrath of God" had been poured out].

In Revelation 16:1–21 (KJV), the Seven Bowls of the "Wrath of God" are poured out onto an unsaved world—upon the whole world—to test those who dwell on the earth.

And I heard a great voice out of the temple saying to the seven angels, Go your ways, and pour out the vials of the Wrath of God upon the earth.

And the first went, and poured out his vial upon the earth [First Bowl of the "Wrath of God"]; and there fell a noisome and grievous sore upon the men which had the mark of the beast, and upon them which worshipped his image.

And the second angel poured out his vial upon the sea [Second Bowl of the "Wrath of God"]; and it became as the blood of a dead man: and every living soul died in the sea.

And the third angel poured out his vial upon the rivers and fountains of waters [Third Bowl of the "Wrath of God"]; and they became blood.

And I heard the angel of the waters say, Thou art righteous, O Lord, which art, and wast, and shalt be, because thou hast judged thus.

For they have shed the blood of saints and prophets, and thou hast given them blood to drink; for they are worthy.

And I heard another out of the altar say, Even so, Lord God Almighty, true and righteous are thy judgments.

And the fourth angel poured out his vial upon the sun [Fourth Bowl of the "Wrath of God"]; and power was given unto him to scorch men with fire. And men were scorched with great heat, and blasphemed the name of God, which hath power over these plagues: and they repented not to give him glory.

And the fifth angel poured out his vial upon the seat of the beast [Fifth Bowl of the "Wrath of God"]; and his kingdom was full of darkness; and they gnawed their tongues for pain, and blasphemed the God of heaven because of their pains and their sores, and repented not of their deeds.

And the sixth angel poured out his vial upon the great river Euphrates [Sixth Bowl of the "Wrath of God"]; and the water thereof was dried up, that the way of the kings of the east might be prepared.

And I saw three unclean spirits like frogs come out of the mouth of the dragon [Satan], and out of the mouth of the beast [the Antichrist], and out of the mouth of the false prophet [the False Prophet].

For they are the spirits of devils, working miracles, which go forth unto the kings of the earth and of the whole world, to gather them to the battle of that great day of God Almighty [demonic spirits convince the kings of the earth and of the whole world to gather their armies to fight Jesus—at the Battle of Armageddon].

Behold, I come as a thief. Blessed is he that watcheth, and keepeth his garments, lest he walk naked, and they see his shame.

And he gathered them together into a place called in the Hebrew tongue Armageddon.

And the seventh angel poured out his vial into the air [Seventh Bowl of the "Wrath of God"]; and there came a great voice out of the temple of heaven, from the throne, saying, "It is done".

And there were voices, and thunders, and lightnings; and there was a great earthquake, such as was not since men were upon the earth, so mighty an earthquake, and so great.

And the great city was divided into three parts, and the cities of the nations fell: and great Babylon came in remembrance before God, to give unto her the cup of the wine of the fierceness of his Wrath [Babylon receives the "Fierceness of the Wrath of God" and this occurs prior to the Battle of Armageddon. Both the (prophesied) "Destruction of Babylon" and the (prophesied) victory of the "Battle of Armageddon" take place during the time period of the Seven Bowls of the "Wrath of God"].

And every island fled away, and the mountains were not found.

And there fell upon men a great hail out of heaven, every stone about the weight of a talent [approximately 70 pounds]: and men blasphemed God because of the plague of the hail; for the plague thereof was exceeding great.

In Revelation 17:1–18 (KJV), John is shown the destruction of Babylon.

And there came one of the seven angels which had the seven vials, and talked with me, saying unto me, Come hither; I will shew unto thee the judgment of the great whore [Babylon] that sitteth upon many waters: With whom the kings of the earth have committed fornication, and the inhabitants of the earth have been made drunk with the wine of her fornication.

So he carried me away in the spirit into the wilderness: and I saw a woman [Babylon] sit upon a scarlet coloured beast [Satan], full of names of blasphemy, having seven heads and ten horns. [In Revelation 12:3—Satan was described as "a great, fiery red dragon having seven heads and ten horns, and seven diadems on his heads." Then we are told in Revelation 12:9 that "the great dragon"—described in Revelation 12:3—was "that serpent of old, called the Devil and Satan."]

And the woman [Babylon] was arrayed in purple and scarlet colour, and decked with gold and precious stones and pearls, having a golden cup in her hand full of abominations and filthiness of her fornication: And upon her forehead was a name written,

MYSTERY,
BABYLON THE GREAT,
THE MOTHER OF HARLOTS AND ABOMINATIONS OF THE EARTH.

And I saw the woman [Babylon] drunken with the blood of the saints, and with the blood of the martyrs of Jesus: and when I saw her, I wondered with great admiration.

And the angel said unto me, Wherefore didst thou marvel? I will tell thee the mystery of the woman [Babylon], and of the beast [Satan] that carrieth her, which hath the seven heads and ten horns.

The beast [Satan] that thou sawest was, and is not; and shall ascend out of the bottomless pit [Satan will be bound and thrown into a bottomless pit for 1,000 years. At the end of the 1,000 years, Satan will be "released" and will ascend out of that bottomless pit], and go into perdition [Satan will ultimately be cast in the Lake of Fire]: and they that dwell on the earth shall wonder, whose names were not written in the Book of Life from the foundation of the world, when they behold the beast [Satan] that was, and is not, and yet is.

And here is the mind which hath wisdom. The seven heads are seven mountains, on which the woman sitteth [These seven mountains may be a reference to the seven kingdoms who have ruled over Israel throughout history: Egypt, Assyria, Babylon, Persia, Greece, Rome, and the (future) kingdom of the Antichrist]. And there are seven kings [This may be a reference to the kings of those same seven kingdoms]: five are fallen [Egypt, Assyria, Babylon, Persia, and Greece all ruled over Israel prior to John writing Revelation], and one is [The Roman Empire currently ruled over Israel during the time when John wrote Revelation], and the other is not yet come [The kingdom of the Antichrist has not yet come]; and when he [the Antichrist] cometh, he must continue a short space.

And the beast [Satan] that was, and is not, even he is the eighth, and is of the seven, and goeth into perdition [Satan is "of the seven"—since he was the one inspiring these seven kingdoms as they came against God and the people of God. Satan is "himself also the eighth"—since when he is "released" from his 1,000 years imprisonment in the bottomless pit, he will go out to deceive the nations and will gather a massive number of people who choose to follow him instead of Jesus. Satan will personally lead this massive group to battle—to fight Jesus and His disciples at Jerusalem—at the end of the 1,000 year period. Satan will lose that battle and will ultimately be cast into the Lake of Fire].

And the ten horns which thou sawest are ten kings, which have received no kingdom as yet; but receive power as kings one hour with the beast [The Ten Kings will follow the Antichrist].

These have one mind, and shall give their power and strength unto the beast [The Ten Kings will follow the Antichrist].

These shall make war with the Lamb [Jesus], and the Lamb [Jesus] shall overcome them: for he [Jesus] is Lord of lords, and King of kings: and they that are with him [those with Jesus] are called, and chosen, and faithful.

> And he saith unto me, the waters which thou sawest, where the whore [Babylon] sitteth, are peoples, and multitudes, and nations, and tongues.
>
> And the ten horns which thou sawest upon the beast [Satan], these shall hate the whore [Babylon], and shall make her desolate and naked, and shall eat her flesh, and burn her [Babylon] with fire [The Ten Kings will destroy Babylon].
>
> For God hath put in their hearts [the hearts of the Ten Kings] to fulfil his will [God's will], and to agree, and give their kingdom unto the beast [the Antichrist], until the words of God shall be fulfilled [The Ten Kings will destroy Babylon and will follow the Antichrist].
>
> And the woman [Babylon] which thou sawest is that great city [Babylon], which reigneth over the kings of the earth.

In Revelation 18:1–24 (KJV), John is given more detail regarding the "Destruction of Babylon"—which was prophesied throughout the Old Testament.

> And after these things I saw another angel come down from heaven, having great power; and the earth was lightened with his glory.
>
> And he cried mightily with a strong voice, saying, Babylon the great is fallen, is fallen, and is become the habitation of devils, and the hold of every foul spirit, and a cage of every unclean and hateful bird.
>
> For all nations have drunk of the wine of the wrath of her fornication, and the kings of the earth have committed fornication with her [Babylon], and the merchants of the earth are waxed rich through the abundance of her delicacies [Babylon's luxury].

And I heard another voice from heaven, saying, Come out of her, my people, that ye be not partakers of her sins, and that ye receive not of her plagues [Babylon's plagues].

For her sins [Babylon's sins] have reached unto heaven, and God hath remembered her iniquities [Babylon's iniquities].

Reward her [Babylon] even as she rewarded you, and double unto her double according to her works: in the cup which she hath filled fill to her double.

How much she [Babylon] hath glorified herself, and lived deliciously, so much torment and sorrow give her: for she [Babylon] saith in her heart, I sit a queen, and am no widow, and shall see no sorrow.

Therefore shall her plagues [Babylon's plagues] come in one day, death, and mourning, and famine; and she [Babylon] shall be utterly burned with fire: for strong is the Lord God who judgeth her [This destruction of Babylon is prophesied throughout the Old Testament].

And the kings of the earth, who have committed fornication and lived deliciously with her, shall bewail her, and lament for her, when they shall see the smoke of her [Babylon's] burning,

Standing afar off for the fear of her torment, saying, Alas, alas that great city Babylon, that mighty city! for in one hour is thy judgment come.

And the merchants of the earth shall weep and mourn over her [Babylon]; for no man buyeth their merchandise any more:

The merchandise of gold, and silver, and precious stones, and of pearls, and fine linen, and purple, and silk, and scarlet, and all thyine wood, and all manner vessels of ivory, and all manner vessels of most precious wood, and of brass, and iron, and marble,

And cinnamon, and odours, and ointments, and frankincense, and wine, and oil, and fine flour, and wheat, and beasts, and sheep, and horses, and chariots, and slaves, and souls of men.

And the fruits that thy soul lusted after are departed from thee, and all things which were dainty and goodly are departed from thee, and thou shalt find them no more at all.

The merchants of these things, which were made rich by her [Babylon], shall stand afar off for the fear of her torment, weeping and wailing,

And saying, Alas, alas that great city [Babylon], that was clothed in fine linen, and purple, and scarlet, and decked with gold, and precious stones, and pearls!

For in one hour so great riches is come to nought. And every shipmaster, and all the company in ships, and sailors, and as many as trade by sea, stood afar off, and cried when they saw the smoke of her [Babylon's] burning, saying, What city is like unto this great city [Babylon]!

And they cast dust on their heads, and cried, weeping and wailing, saying, Alas, alas that great city [Babylon], wherein were made rich all that had ships in the sea by reason of her costliness! for in one hour is she [Babylon] made desolate.

Rejoice over her, thou heaven, and ye holy apostles and prophets; for God hath avenged you on her [Babylon].

> And a mighty angel took up a stone like a great millstone, and cast it into the sea, saying, Thus with violence shall that great city Babylon be thrown down, and shall be found no more at all.
>
> And the voice of harpers, and musicians, and of pipers, and trumpeters, shall be heard no more at all in thee [Babylon]; and no craftsman, of whatsoever craft he be, shall be found any more in thee [Babylon]; and the sound of a millstone shall be heard no more at all in thee;
>
> And the light of a candle shall shine no more at all in thee [Babylon]; and the voice of the bridegroom and of the bride shall be heard no more at all in thee: for thy merchants [the merchants of Babylon] were the great men of the earth; for by thy sorceries were all nations deceived.
>
> And in her [in Babylon] was found the blood of prophets, and of saints, and of all that were slain upon the earth [This destruction of Babylon will fulfill many Old Testament Prophetic Scriptures].

In Revelation 19:1–10 (KJV), after Babylon is destroyed, John is shown the rejoicing in heaven. This is still prior to the Battle of Armageddon.

> And after these things I heard a great voice of much people in heaven, saying, Alleluia; Salvation, and glory, and honour, and power, unto the Lord our God:
>
> For true and righteous are his judgments: for he hath judged the great whore [Babylon], which did corrupt the earth with her fornication, and hath avenged the blood of his servants at her [Babylon's] hand.
>
> And again they said, Alleluia And her smoke [the smoke of Babylon] rose up for ever and ever.

And the four and twenty elders and the four beasts fell down and worshipped God that sat on the throne, saying, Amen; Alleluia.

And a voice came out of the throne, saying, Praise our God, all ye his servants, and ye that fear him, both small and great.

And I heard as it were the voice of a great multitude, and as the voice of many waters, and as the voice of mighty thunderings, saying, Alleluia: for the Lord God omnipotent reigneth.

Let us be glad and rejoice, and give honour to him: for the marriage of the Lamb is come, and his wife hath made herself ready.

And to her was granted that she should be arrayed in fine linen, clean and white: for the fine linen is the righteousness of saints.

And he saith unto me, Write, Blessed are they which are called unto the marriage supper of the Lamb [This "Marriage Supper of the Lamb" may be a reference to the "Feast of Tabernacles" which Jesus will observe with all of His disciples at the Temple in Jerusalem, after the Battle of Armageddon is over and after the Temple is cleansed]. And he saith unto me, These are the true sayings of God.

And I fell at his feet to worship him. And he said unto me, See thou do it not: I am thy fellowservant, and of thy brethren that have the testimony of Jesus: worship God: for the testimony of Jesus is the spirit of prophecy.

In Revelation 19:11–20:3 (KJV), John is shown the Battle of Armageddon.

And I saw heaven opened, and behold a white horse; and he [Jesus] that sat upon him was called Faithful and True, and in righteousness he [Jesus] doth judge and make war.

His eyes were as a flame of fire, and on his head were many crowns; and he [Jesus] had a name written, that no man knew, but he himself.

And he [Jesus] was clothed with a vesture dipped in blood: and his name is called The Word of God.

And the armies which were in heaven followed him [Jesus] upon white horses, clothed in fine linen, white and clean.

And out of his mouth goeth a sharp sword, that with it he [Jesus] should smite the nations: and he [Jesus] shall rule them with a rod of iron: and he [Jesus] treadeth the winepress of the fierceness and Wrath of Almighty God [the Wrath of God].

And he [Jesus] hath on his vesture and on his thigh a name written,

King Of Kings, And Lord Of Lords.

And I saw an angel standing in the sun; and he cried with a loud voice, saying to all the fowls that fly in the midst of heaven, Come and gather yourselves together unto the supper of the great God [This is in preparation for the Battle of Armageddon];

That ye may eat the flesh of kings, and the flesh of captains, and the flesh of mighty men, and the flesh of horses, and of them that sit on them, and the flesh of all men, both free and bond, both small and great [This is in preparation for the Battle of Armageddon].

> And I saw the beast [the Antichrist], and the kings of the earth, and their armies, gathered together to make war against him [Jesus] that sat on the horse, and against his army [the army of Jesus].
>
> And the beast [the Antichrist] was taken, and with him the false prophet [the False Prophet] that wrought miracles before him, with which he [the False Prophet] deceived them that had received the mark of the beast [the Mark of the Antichrist], and them that worshipped his image. These both [the Antichrist and the False Prophet] were cast alive into a Lake of Fire burning with brimstone.
>
> And the remnant were slain with the sword of him [Jesus] that sat upon the horse, which sword proceeded out of his mouth: and all the fowls were filled with their flesh.
>
> And I saw an angel come down from heaven, having the key of the bottomless pit and a great chain in his hand.
>
> And he laid hold on the dragon [Satan], that old serpent, which is the Devil, and Satan, and bound him [Satan] a thousand years, And cast him [Satan] into the bottomless pit, and shut him up, and set a seal upon him, that he [Satan] should deceive the nations no more, till the thousand years should be fulfilled: and after that he must be loosed a little season [The Wrath of God is now over].

In Revelation 20:4–10 (KJV), John is shown the 1,000 year reign of Jesus—who will rule the world from Jerusalem.

> And I saw thrones, and they sat upon them, and judgment was given unto them: and I saw the souls of them that were beheaded for the Witness of Jesus, and for the Word of God, and which had not worshipped the beast [the Antichrist], neither his image [the image of the Antichrist], neither had received his mark [the Mark of

the Antichrist] upon their foreheads, or in their hands; and they lived and reigned with Christ a thousand years [Disciples of Jesus will live and reign with Jesus for 1,000 years—as He rules the earth from Jerusalem].

But the rest of the dead [the "unsaved" dead] lived not again until the thousand years were finished. This is the first resurrection [After the thousand-year period when Jesus rules on the earth—is over—there will be a Judgment Day and all of the "unsaved" dead will be judged].

Blessed and holy is he that hath part in the first resurrection: on such the second death hath no power, but they shall be priests of God and of Christ, and shall reign with him a thousand years [The second death is the "Lake of Fire"].

And when the thousand years are expired, Satan shall be loosed out of his prison, and shall go out to deceive the nations which are in the four quarters of the earth, Gog, and Magog, to gather them together to battle: the number of whom is as the sand of the sea [Satan is able to gather a massive number of people who choose to follow him—instead of Jesus].

And they went up on the breadth of the earth, and compassed the camp of the saints about, and the beloved city [This is a massive number of people who chose to follow Satan—and they go with Satan to attack Jesus at Jerusalem]: and fire came down from God out of heaven, and devoured them [God sends fire from Heaven and devours Satan and those who follow Satan].

And the devil [Satan] that deceived them was cast into the Lake of Fire and brimstone, where the beast and the false prophet are, and [Satan and the Antichrist and the

False Prophet] shall be tormented day and night for ever and ever.

In Revelation 20:11–15 (KJV), John is shown the "Great White Throne" Judgment.

> And I saw a great white throne, and him that sat on it, from whose face the earth and the heaven fled away; and there was found no place for them.
>
> And I saw the dead, small and great, stand before God; and the books were opened: and another book was opened, which is the Book of Life: and the dead were judged out of those things which were written in the books, according to their works.
>
> And the sea gave up the dead which were in it; and death and hell delivered up the dead which were in them: and they were judged every man according to their works.
>
> And death and hell were cast into the Lake of Fire. This is the second death [The "Lake of Fire" is the "Second Death"].
>
> And whosoever was not found written in the Book of Life was cast into the Lake of Fire.

In Revelation 21:1–22:21 (KJV), John is shown the "New Heaven" and the "New Earth".

> And I saw a new heaven and a new earth: for the first heaven and the first earth were passed away; and there was no more sea.
>
> And I John saw the holy city, new Jerusalem, coming down from God out of heaven, prepared as a bride adorned for her husband.

And I heard a great voice out of heaven saying, Behold, the tabernacle of God is with men, and he will dwell with them, and they shall be his people, and God himself shall be with them, and be their God.

And God shall wipe away all tears from their eyes; and there shall be no more death, neither sorrow, nor crying, neither shall there be any more pain: for the former things are passed away.

And he that sat upon the throne said, Behold, I make all things new. And he said unto me, Write: for these words are true and faithful.

And he said unto me, It is done. I am Alpha and Omega, the beginning and the end. I will give unto him that is athirst of the fountain of the Water of Life freely.

He that overcometh [the "Disciples of Jesus" who are "Faithful unto Death"] shall inherit all things; and I will be his God, and he shall be my son.

But the fearful, and unbelieving, and the abominable, and murderers, and whoremongers, and sorcerers, and idolaters, and all liars, shall have their part in the lake which burneth with fire and brimstone [the Lake of Fire]: which is the second death [the "Lake of Fire" is the "Second Death"].

And there came unto me one of the seven angels which had the seven vials full of the seven last plagues [one of the Angels who had one of the Seven Bowls of the "Wrath of God"], and talked with me, saying, Come hither, I will shew thee the bride, the Lamb's wife.

And he carried me away in the spirit to a great and high mountain, and shewed me that great city, the holy Jerusalem, descending out of heaven from God,

Having the glory of God: and her light was like unto a stone most precious, even like a jasper stone, clear as crystal;

And had a wall great and high, and had twelve gates, and at the gates twelve angels, and names written thereon, which are the names of the twelve tribes of the children of Israel:

On the east three gates; on the north three gates; on the south three gates; and on the west three gates.

And the wall of the city had twelve foundations, and in them the names of the twelve apostles of the Lamb.

And he that talked with me had a golden reed to measure the city, and the gates thereof, and the wall thereof.

And the city lieth foursquare, and the length is as large as the breadth: and he measured the city with the reed, twelve thousand furlongs. The length and the breadth and the height of it are equal.

And he measured the wall thereof, an hundred and forty and four cubits, according to the measure of a man, that is, of the angel.

And the building of the wall of it was of jasper: and the city was pure gold, like unto clear glass.

And the foundations of the wall of the city were garnished with all manner of precious stones. The first foundation was jasper; the second, sapphire; the third, a chalcedony; the fourth, an emerald;

The fifth, sardonyx; the sixth, sardius; the seventh, chrysolyte; the eighth, beryl; the ninth, a topaz; the tenth, a chrysoprasus; the eleventh, a jacinth; the twelfth, an amethyst.

And the twelve gates were twelve pearls: every several gate was of one pearl: and the street of the city was pure gold, as it were transparent glass.

And I saw no temple therein: for the Lord God Almighty and the Lamb [Jesus] are the temple of it.

And the city ["New Jerusalem"] had no need of the sun, neither of the moon, to shine in it: for the glory of God did lighten it, and the Lamb [Jesus] is the light thereof.

And the nations of them which are saved [Christians—Disciples of Jesus] shall walk in the light of it: and the kings of the earth do bring their glory and honour into it.

And the gates of it shall not be shut at all by day: for there shall be no night there.

And they shall bring the glory and honour of the nations into it.

And there shall in no wise enter into it any thing that defileth, neither whatsoever worketh abomination, or maketh a lie: but they which are written in the Lamb's Book of Life [Only those whose names are written in the Lamb's Book of Life are allowed to enter New Jerusalem. Those whose names were NOT found written in the Lamb's Book of Life were cast into the Lake of Fire].

And he shewed me a pure river of Water of Life, clear as crystal, proceeding out of the throne of God and of the Lamb [Jesus].

In the midst of the street of it, and on either side of the river, was there the Tree of Life [This Tree of Life was also in the Garden of Eden], which bare twelve manner of fruits, and yielded her fruit every month: and the leaves of the tree were for the healing of the nations.

And there shall be no more curse: but the throne of God and of the Lamb [Jesus] shall be in it; and his servants shall serve him:

And they shall see his face; and his name shall be in their foreheads.

And there shall be no night there; and they need no candle, neither light of the sun; for the Lord God giveth them light: and they shall reign for ever and ever.

And he said unto me, These sayings are faithful and true: and the Lord God of the holy prophets sent his angel to shew unto his servants the things which must shortly be done [God has given us Revelation—so that we might read and understand].

Behold, I come quickly: blessed is he that keepeth the sayings of the prophecy of this book [Blessed is he who is "Faithful unto Death"].

And I John saw these things, and heard them. And when I had heard and seen, I fell down to worship before the feet of the angel which shewed me these things.

Then saith he unto me, See thou do it not: for I am thy fellowservant, and of thy brethren the prophets, and of them which keep the sayings of this book: worship God.

And he saith unto me, Seal not the sayings of the prophecy of this book: for the time is at hand.

He that is unjust, let him be unjust still: and he which is filthy, let him be filthy still: and he that is righteous, let him be righteous still: and he that is holy, let him be holy still.

And, behold, I [Jesus] come quickly; and my reward is with me, to give every man according as his work shall be.

I [Jesus] am Alpha and Omega, the beginning and the end, the first and the last.

Blessed are they that do his commandments, that they may have right to the Tree of Life, and may enter in through the gates into the city ["New Jerusalem"].

For without are dogs, and sorcerers, and whoremongers, and murderers, and idolaters, and whosoever loveth and maketh a lie [These are those who are in the Lake of Fire].

I Jesus have sent mine angel to testify unto you these things in the churches. I am the root and the offspring of David, and the bright and morning star.

And the Spirit and the bride say, Come. And let him that heareth say, Come. And let him that is athirst come. And whosoever will, let him take the Water of Life freely.

For I testify unto every man that heareth the words of the prophecy of this book, If any man shall add unto these things, God shall add unto him the plagues that are written in this book:

And if any man shall take away from the words of the book of this prophecy, God shall take away his part out of the Book of Life, and out of the holy city, and from the things which are written in this book.

He which testifieth these things saith, Surely I come quickly.

Amen.

Even so, come, Lord Jesus.

The grace of our Lord Jesus Christ be with you all.

Amen.

The biblical "Sequence of Events" mentioned in Revelation—beginning with the "Wrath of God" and ending with the "New Heaven" and the "New Earth"—is as follows.

- The Rapture has just occurred.
- All disciples of Jesus are now with Jesus in Heaven.
- The earth is now inhabited by demons and unsaved people.
- Seven Angels are given the Seven Bowls of the "Wrath of God"—Revelation 15:1–8.
- First Bowl of the "Wrath of God"—A foul and loathsome sore came upon those who had the Mark of the Beast and upon those who worshipped his image—Revelation 16:1–21.
- Second Bowl of the "Wrath of God"—The sea became blood as of a dead man, and every living creature in the sea died—Revelation 16:1–21.
- Third Bowl of the "Wrath of God"—Rivers and springs of water became blood—Revelation 16:1–21.
- John heard one from the altar saying, "Even so, Lord God Almighty, true and righteous are Your judgments"—Revelation 16:1–21.
- Fourth Bowl of the "Wrath of God"—People were scorched with great heat and with fire; they did not repent and they blasphemed the name of God—Revelation 16:1–21.
- Fifth Bowl of the "Wrath of God"—The kingdom of the Antichrist became full of darkness, and they gnawed their tongues because

of the pain. They did not repent, and they blasphemed God because of their pains and sores—Revelation 16:1–21.
- Sixth Bowl of the "Wrath of God"—The Euphrates River was dried up to make it easy for the kings of the east to come to Jerusalem to fight Jesus at the Battle of Armageddon—Revelation 16:1–21.
- John sees three unclean spirits coming out of the mouths of Satan, the Antichrist, and the False Prophet. These demons deceive the kings of the earth to gather with their armies to fight Jesus at the Battle of Armageddon—Revelation 16:1–21.
- Seventh Bowl of the "Wrath of God"—Noises, thunderings, lightnings, and a great earthquake as had not occurred since men were on the earth. Every island fled away, and the mountains were not found. Great Babylon was remembered before God, to give her the cup of the wine of the fierceness of His Wrath. Great hail fell upon men and each hailstone weighed about seventy pounds each. Men blasphemed God because of the plague of the hail, since that plague was exceedingly great—Revelation 16:1–21.
- John is shown—in detail—the destruction of Babylon and exactly how Babylon receives the "Fierceness of the Wrath of God." In Babylon was found the blood of the prophets and saints and of all who were slain on earth. God repays Babylon double. Babylon is made desolate and shall not be found anymore. This destruction of Babylon will fulfill many Old Testament prophecies. Babylon is fallen, is fallen! Strong is the Lord God who judges Babylon—Revelation 17:1–19:10.
- The Battle of Armageddon—Jesus is victorious—Revelation 19:11–20:3.
- The Antichrist and the False Prophet are thrown alive into the Lake of Fire—Revelation 19:11–20:3.
- The rest are killed with the sword that proceeds from the mouth of Jesus [the Word of God] —Revelation 19:11–20:3.
- Satan is bound and is thrown into a bottomless pit for 1,000 years—Revelation 19:11–20:3.
- This is the end of the "Wrath of God"—Revelation 19:11–20:3.
- Jesus begins to rule on the earth for 1,000 years from Jerusalem.

- Christians live and reign with Jesus—as Kings and Priests—during the thousand-year period—Revelation 20:4–10.
- When the 1,000 years have expired, Satan is released from the bottomless pit—Revelation 20:4–10.
- Satan goes out to deceive all the nations and is able to deceive many people who choose to follow Satan instead of Jesus—Revelation 20:4–10.
- Satan gathers an army for battle—whose number is as the sand of the sea—Revelation 20:4–10.
- Satan and his army surround Jerusalem and prepare to attack Jesus—Revelation 20:4–10.
- Fire comes down from God and devours Satan and his army—Revelation 20:4–10.
- Satan is cast into the Lake of Fire, where the Antichrist and the False Prophet are—Revelation 20:4–10.
- Satan and the Antichrist and the False Prophet are tormented day and night forever—in the Lake of Fire—Revelation 20:4–10.
- The "Great White Throne" Judgment. All the unsaved dead are judged according to their works—Revelation 20:11–15.
- Anyone whose name is not found written in the Book of Life is cast into the Lake of Fire—Revelation 20:11–15.
- All of the unsaved dead are cast into the Lake of Fire—Revelation 20:11–15.
- Death and Hades are cast into the Lake of Fire—Revelation 20:11–15.
- The Lake of Fire is the Second Death—Revelation 20:11–15.
- Only those whose names are written in the Book of Life are allowed to enter the "New Jerusalem"—Revelation 21:1–22:21.
- There is a "New Heaven" and a "New Earth"—Revelation 21:1–22:21.

Jesus instructs His disciples to "Stand" and to "Overcome" and to be "Faithful unto Death". Therefore, it is important for a disciple of Jesus to understand this Bible Truth:

> **TRIBULATION** and **PERSECUTION**
> come from our **STAND**
> on the **WORD of GOD** and our **TESTIMONY of JESUS**.

As we read the first three verses of the Book of Revelation, it is easy to see that the LORD definitely wants us to understand the actual biblical sequence of these end-time events. God shows everything to Jesus, who sends His angel to show everything to His servant John, who writes a book, so that we—even two thousand years later—can read and understand the actual biblical sequence of these end-time events. The LORD wants us to understand!

> The Revelation of Jesus Christ, which God gave Him [Jesus] to show His servants—things which must shortly take place. And He [Jesus] sent and signified it by His angel to His servant John, who bore witness to the Word of God, and to the Testimony of Jesus Christ, to all things that he saw.
>
> Blessed is he who reads and those who hear the words of this prophecy, and keep those things which are written in it; for the time is near. (Revelation 1:1–3)

CHAPTER 8

Understanding the Biblical Sequence of Events

Putting the entire sequence together, we get a clear picture of "What Does the Bible Say?" This is the actual biblical "Sequence of Events" that we have seen so far.

- Jesus, the Messiah, accomplishes what He was sent to the earth to accomplish during His first coming: "For God so loved the world that He gave His only begotten Son, that whoever believes in Him should not perish but have everlasting life"—John 3:16.
- You and I now have the opportunity to become disciples of Jesus.

   > But what does it [the Scripture] say? "The WORD is near you, in your Mouth and in your Heart"—that is the Word of Faith which we preach—that if you confess with your mouth the Lord Jesus and believe in your heart that God has raised Him from the dead—you will be Saved. For with the heart one believes unto Righteousness, and with the mouth confession is made unto Salvation—Romans 10:8–10.

- Jesus commands His disciples to be "Faithful unto Death"— Matthew 16:25; Mark 8:35; Luke 9:24; John 12:25.
- Beginnings of Sorrows—This could have begun as early as when Jesus ascended to heaven because there certainly have been wars,

rumors of wars, earthquakes, etc. since that time—Matthew 24:3–13; Mark 13:3–13.
- The disciples of Jesus began to be persecuted and were "Faithful unto Death".

> And they stoned Stephen as he was calling on God and saying, "Lord Jesus, receive my spirit." Then he knelt down and cried out with a loud voice, "Lord, do not charge them with this sin." And when he had said this, he fell asleep. Now Saul [who later became the great "Apostle Paul"] was consenting to his death. At that time a great persecution arose against the church which was at Jerusalem; and they were all scattered throughout the regions of Judea and Samaria, except the apostles. And devout men carried Stephen to his burial, and made great lamentation over him. As for Saul, he made havoc of the church, entering every house, and dragging off men and women, committing them to prison. Therefore those who were scattered went everywhere preaching the WORD—Acts 7:59–8:4.

- The Temple and Jerusalem are destroyed in AD 70 by the Roman Empire; over one million are killed, and the children of Israel are scattered throughout the earth in exile and without a homeland. Israel ceases to exist as a nation for almost 2,000 years.
- The children of Israel continue to endure God's "Four Severe Judgments"—the sword, famine, wild beasts, and pestilence. Israel endures over 2,500 years of God's punishment for the iniquity of the nation of Israel beginning with its seventy-year captivity in Babylon during the time of Daniel and continuing through the years of the World War II Holocaust—which ended in 1945. Israel endures over 2,500 years of God's punishment for the "Persistent Unfaithfulness of Israel"—Ezekiel 4:1–6; Leviticus 26:18–28.
- Israel becomes a nation (again) in 1948; that ends the over 2,500 years of God's punishment for the "Persistent Unfaithfulness of Israel". God honors His promise and returns Israel to its homeland in 1948.

At some point in the future,

- God takes the Scroll in His right hand; He is ready to start the final seven years and fulfill ALL of His promises to Israel—Revelation 5:1; Daniel 9:20–27.
- Jesus takes the Scroll from the hand of God—Revelation 5:7.
- There is a seven-year covenant with many—which may give the nation of Israel an opportunity to rebuild the Temple (if the Temple has not already been rebuilt by that time)—Daniel 9:20–27.
- Jesus opens the First Seal to start the "Seven-year Tribulation"—Revelation 6:1.
- Tribulation begins and continues—Matthew 24:3–13.
- The "Seven-year Tribulation" is God's punishment for the "Persistent Unfaithfulness of the World". This is seven years of what God calls His "Four Severe Judgments"—the sword, famine, wild beasts, and pestilence. Since Christians are in the world, Christians will experience what the world experiences and Christians will endure what the world endures—during the "Seven-year Tribulation".
- God will use these final seven years to fulfill ALL of His promises to Israel—Daniel 9:20–27.
- Temple is rebuilt—the Bible does not tell us whether the Temple is rebuilt before the Tribulation begins, but the Temple is definitely rebuilt before the Antichrist commits the Abomination of Desolation—Matthew 24:15–22; Mark 13:14–20; 2 Thessalonians 2:1–5.
- First Seal—one on a white horse was given a crown and he went out conquering and to conquer—Revelation 6:1–8.
- Second Seal—one on a red horse takes peace from earth—that people should kill one another—Revelation 6:1–8.
- Third Seal—one on a black horse with a pair of scales in his hand—a quart of wheat for a denarius and 3 quarts of barley for a denarius—economic hard times—Revelation 6:1–8.
- Fourth Seal—one on a pale horse whose name is Death, followed by Hades—power was given to them over a fourth of the earth—to kill with the sword, hunger, death, and by the beasts of the earth—Revelation 6:1–8.

- Suppose for example that there were a total of eight billion people living on the earth at that time. Since a fourth of the earth is killed, then that would mean that approximately two billion people will be killed during this first three and a half year period—during the first three and a half years of the "Seven-year Tribulation".
- Fifth Seal—John sees under the altar [in heaven] the souls of those who had been slain [killed] for the Word of God and for their Testimony [These are disciples of Jesus who were Faithful unto Death]—Revelation 6:9–11.
- Sixth Seal—great earthquake, the sun becomes black as sackcloth, the moon becomes like blood, stars fall, and the sky recedes like a scroll when it is rolled up, and every mountain and island is moved out of its place—Revelation 6:12–17.
- During this time, people think that this is the "Wrath of the Lamb". Nevertheless, this is NOT the "Wrath of God"; this is still during the first three and a half years of the "Seven-year Tribulation"—Revelation 6:12–17.
- Prior to the Seventh Seal—but still during the Sixth Seal—the 144,000 are sealed. These 144,000 are the 12,000 each from twelve tribes of Israel. These 144,000 are "hand picked" and "set apart" and "sealed"—but they are not yet "Saved"—they are not yet "Disciples of Jesus"—Revelation 7:1–17.
- Seventh Seal—there is silence in heaven for about half an hour—and the seven angels who stand before God are given Seven Trumpets—Revelation 8:1–6.
- An angel with a golden censer is given much incense and offers it with the prayers of the saints upon the altar, which is before the throne in heaven—Revelation 8:1–6.
- The angel fills the censer with fire from the altar and throws it to the earth. There are noises, thunderings, lightnings, and an earthquake—Revelation 8:1–6.
- The angels with the Seven Trumpets prepare to sound—Revelation 8:1–6.
- First Trumpet—hail and fire mingled with blood are thrown to the earth. A third of the trees are burned up and all green grass is burned up—Revelation 8:7–13.

- Second Trumpet—something like a great mountain burning with fire is thrown into the sea—a third of the sea becomes blood; a third of the creatures in the sea die; a third of all ships are destroyed—Revelation 8:7–13.
- Third Trumpet—a great star fell from heaven burning like a torch, and it fell on a third of the rivers and on the springs of water. The name of the star is Wormwood. A third of the waters became wormwood, and many men died from the water, because it was made bitter—Revelation 8:7–13.
- Fourth Trumpet—a third of the sun was struck, a third of the moon, and a third of the stars, so that a third of them were darkened. A third of the day did not shine, and likewise the night—Revelation 8:7–13.
- An angel flying through the midst of heaven says in a loud voice, "<u>Woe, Woe, Woe</u> to the inhabitants of the earth, because of the remaining blasts of the trumpet of the three angels who are about to sound." In other words, the Fifth Trumpet is given the name "First Woe"; the Sixth Trumpet is given the name "Second Woe"; and the Seventh Trumpet is given the name "Third Woe"—Revelation 8:7–13.
- Fifth Trumpet (the First Woe)—the bottomless pit is opened and demonic beings called locusts are given authority to harm all but the 144,000. They are given power to torment for five months. Nevertheless, they are not given authority to kill. People will seek death because of this torment, but death will flee from them—Revelation 9:1–12.
- This five month torment during the time of the Fifth Trumpet may be what Jeremiah was referring to when he spoke of "Jacob's Trouble".

> Ask now and see, whether a man is ever in labor with child? So why do I see every man with his hands on his loins like a woman in labor, and all faces turned pale? Alas! For that day is great, so that none is like it: and it is the time of "Jacob's Trouble", but he shall be saved out of it—Jeremiah 30:6–7.

- The 144,000 "shall be saved out of it"—since they are protected from the five month torment. These 144,000 are 12,000 each from twelve tribes of Israel. These 144,000 have been "hand picked" and "set apart" and "sealed"—but they are not yet "Saved"—they are not yet "Disciples of Jesus"—Revelation 7:1–17.
- Revelation 9:12 is the end of the Fifth Trumpet (the First Woe).
- Revelation 9:12 is the approximate end of the first three and a half years of the "Seven-year Tribulation".
- Prior to when the Sixth Trumpet (the Second Woe) sounds in Revelation 9:13—the following events will have already taken place—during the first three and a half years of the "Seven-year Tribulation".

  o The Antichrist is now firmly in power and is operating as a world leader—Daniel 9:20–27.
  o Approximately one fourth of the population of the earth has been killed during the first half of the "Seven-Year Tribulation"—Revelation 6:1–9:12.
  o Many disciples of Jesus were "Faithful unto Death" and were martyred for their stand on the Word of God and for their Testimony of Jesus—Revelation 6:9–11.
  o The Temple has been rebuilt—Daniel 9:20–27.
  o The "Daily Sacrifices" at the Temple have begun—Daniel 9:20–27.
  o The 144,000 of the Twelve Tribes of Israel have already been "Sealed". These 144,000 were "hand-picked" and "set apart" and "sealed"—but they are not yet "Saved"—they are not yet "Disciples of Jesus"—Revelation 7:1–17.
  o God has promised throughout the Old Testament Scriptures and the New Testament Scriptures that "Israel will be saved". Nevertheless, Israel must be "saved" the same way any person is "saved". Paul taught that an individual is saved by grace through faith. Consider Ephesians 2:8–9: "For by grace you have been saved through faith, and that not of yourselves; it is the gift of God, not of works, lest anyone should boast."

In Romans 10:8–13, Paul taught the following.

> But what does it [the Scripture] say? "The word is near you, in your mouth and in your heart" (that is, the word of faith which we preach): that if you confess with your mouth the Lord Jesus and believe in your heart that God has raised Him from the dead, you will be saved. For with the heart one believes unto righteousness, and with the mouth confession is made unto salvation. For the Scripture says, "Whoever believes on Him will not be put to shame." For there is no distinction between Jew and Greek [the 144,000 must be "Saved" the same way that anyone is "Saved"], for the same Lord over all is rich to all who call upon Him. For "whoever calls on the name of the Lord shall be saved."

- Revelation 9:13 is the beginning of the Sixth Trumpet (the Second Woe).
- Revelation 9:13 is the approximate beginning of the second three and a half years of the "Seven-year Tribulation".
- Temple is rebuilt—the Bible does not tell us whether the Temple is rebuilt before the Tribulation begins, but the Temple is definitely rebuilt before the Antichrist stops the "Daily Sacrifices" at the Temple—Daniel 9:20–27.
- The Antichrist enters Jerusalem with an army and Stops the Daily Sacrifices at the Temple—Daniel 9:20–27. This event is the "starting point" of a countdown for four important end-time events. Consider this event as day 0.
- After day 0—in other words, after the Antichrist has Stopped the Daily Sacrifices at the Temple, the two witnesses [the Two Prophets] will appear and will minister to the 144,000 for 1,260 days—during the time period of the Sixth Trumpet. They will teach "Jesus is the Messiah" to the 144,000—and to all others who will come to hear the Word of God—at the Temple—in Jerusalem—for three and a half years—Revelation 11:1–14.

- During the 1,260-day—three and a half year—ministry of the Two Prophets, every single one of the 144,000 will be saved—12,000 each from the twelve tribes of Israel will be saved—and every single one will become a disciple of Jesus. In fact, every single one of these 144,000 will be "Faithful unto Death" and we will see them in Heaven—during the Seventh Trumpet—<u>prior to the Rapture</u>—and they are described as "ones who follow the Lamb wherever He goes"—Revelation 14:1–5.
- Therefore, Israel will be saved—and God's promise to save Israel will be fulfilled—and all of this will occur <u>prior to the Rapture</u>—prior to the end of the Seventh Trumpet—Revelation 14:1–5.
- The tremendous power of the Two Prophets will prevent the Antichrist from committing the "Abomination of Desolation" during their three and a half year ministry—Revelation 11:1–14.
- Revelation 11:14 is the end the Sixth Trumpet (the Second Woe).
- Prior to when the Seventh Trumpet (the Third Woe) sounds in Revelation 11:15—the following events will have already taken place.

    o Approximately one fourth of the population of the earth will have been killed during the first half of the "Seven-Year Tribulation"—Revelation 6:1–9:12.
    o Another approximately one third of the population of the earth will have been killed during the second half of the "Seven-year Tribulation"—Revelation 9:13–11:14.
    o This means that approximately one half of the total population of the earth was killed in the previous seven years—Revelation 9:13–11:14.
    o The 144,000 are now all "Saved" and are all "Disciples of Jesus"—Revelation 14:1–5.
    o The Two Prophets have now been killed—Revelation 11:1–14.

- Revelation 11:15 is the beginning of the Seventh Trumpet (the Third Woe).
- On day 1,290—in other words, one thousand two hundred and ninety days after the Antichrist has <u>Stopped the Daily Sacrifices at the Temple</u>—the Antichrist will enter the Holy of Holies in the

- Temple and commit the "Abomination of Desolation"—Daniel 12:4-13.
- Abomination of Desolation—This is where the Antichrist goes into the Holy of Holies—in the Temple in Jerusalem—and sits as God—in the Temple of God—and proclaims that he [the Antichrist] is God. This is the event that the Bible refers to as the "Abomination of Desolation"—Daniel 12:4-13; Matthew 24:15-22; Mark 13:14-20; 2 Thessalonians 2:1-5.
- Great Tribulation—In Matthew 24:21-22, Jesus said, "For then there will be <u>Great Tribulation</u>, such as has not been since the beginning of the world until this time, no, nor ever shall be. And unless those days were shortened, no flesh would be saved; but for the elect's sake those days will be shortened".
- In Matthew, Jesus referred to the time toward the end of the Tribulation as the "Great Tribulation". This is the time immediately after the Abomination of Desolation and just before the Rapture. This is the time period that Jesus referred to where <u>it has never been that bad before</u> and where <u>it will never be that bad again</u>—Matthew 24:15-22; Mark 13:14-20; Matthew 24:29-31; Mark 13:24-27.
- During this time period of the Seventh Trumpet (the Third Woe)—the "False Prophet" will decree that every single person living on the earth will be required to take the "Mark of the Beast" or be killed. This will create a time where <u>it has never been that bad before</u> and where <u>it will never be that bad again</u>—Revelation 12:1-14:20.
- An Angel Preaches the Gospel to those on the earth prior to the Rapture—Revelation 14:6-7.
- A second Angel follows and says, "Babylon is fallen, is fallen, that great city, because she has made all nations drink of the wine of the wrath of her fornication"—Revelation 14:8.
- A third Angel followed them, saying with a loud voice, "If anyone worships the beast [the Antichrist], and receives his mark on his forehead or on his hand [the Mark of the Antichrist], he himself shall also drink of the wine of the Wrath of God [the Wrath of God] which is poured out full strength into the cup of His indignation. He shall be tormented with fire and brimstone in

the presence of the holy angels and in the presence of the Lamb. And the smoke of their torment ascends forever and ever; and they shall have no rest day or night, who worship the beast [the Antichrist] and his image [the image of the Antichrist], and whoever receives the mark of his name" [whoever receives the Mark of the Antichrist]—Revelation 14:9–11.

- Sun and moon are darkened—Matthew 24:29–31; Mark 13:24–27.
- Last Trumpet—1 Corinthians 15:51–52.
- Jesus descends from heaven with a shout, with the voice of an archangel, and with the Trumpet of God—1 Thessalonians 4:15–18.
- Son of Man coming on the clouds—Matthew 24:29–31; Mark 13:24–27; Revelation 14:14–20.
- On day 1,335—in other words, one thousand three hundred and thirty-five days after the Antichrist has <u>Stopped the Daily Sacrifices at the Temple</u>—the Bible says that he who waits and comes to the one thousand three hundred and thirty-five days will be "Blessed". When we subtract 1,290 from 1,335, we can understand that this event will occur approximately 45 days after the "Abomination of Desolation" [which occurs inside the Temple]. This event appears to be the exact same event that Jesus referred to in Matthew 24:15–22, Mark 13:14–20, Matthew 24:29–31, and Mark 13:24–27. This event is known as the "Rapture"—Daniel 12:4-13.
- Rapture—Matthew 24:15–22; Mark 13:14–20; Matthew 24:29–31; Mark 13:24–27; 1 Corinthians 15:51–52; 1 Thessalonians 4:15–18; Revelation 14:14–20.
- All disciples of Jesus are now with Jesus in Heaven.
- The earth is now inhabited by demons and unsaved people.
- Wrath of God—Revelation 14:14–20.
- Seven Angels are given the Seven Bowls of the "Wrath of God"—Revelation 15:1–8.
- First Bowl of the "Wrath of God"—A foul and loathsome sore came upon those who had the Mark of the Beast and upon those who worshipped his image—Revelation 16:1–21.
- Second Bowl of the "Wrath of God"—The sea became blood as of a dead man, and every living creature in the sea died—Revelation 16:1–21.

- Third Bowl of the "Wrath of God"—Rivers and springs of water became blood—Revelation 16:1–21.
- John heard one from the altar saying, "Even so, Lord God Almighty, true and righteous are Your judgments"—Revelation 16:1–21.
- Fourth Bowl of the "Wrath of God"—People were scorched with great heat and with fire; they did not repent and they blasphemed the name of God—Revelation 16:1–21.
- Fifth Bowl of the "Wrath of God"—The kingdom of the Antichrist became full of darkness, and they gnawed their tongues because of the pain. They did not repent, and they blasphemed God because of their pains and sores—Revelation 16:1–21.
- Sixth Bowl of the "Wrath of God"—The Euphrates River was dried up to make it easy for the kings of the east to come to Jerusalem to fight Jesus at the Battle of Armageddon—Revelation 16:1–21.
- John sees three unclean spirits coming out of the mouths of Satan, the Antichrist, and the False Prophet. These demons deceive the kings of the earth to gather with their armies to fight Jesus at the Battle of Armageddon—Revelation 16:1–21.
- Seventh Bowl of the "Wrath of God"—Noises, thunderings, lightnings, and a great earthquake as had not occurred since men were on the earth. Every island fled away, and the mountains were not found. Great Babylon was remembered before God, to give her the cup of the wine of the fierceness of His Wrath. Great hail fell upon men and each hailstone weighed about seventy pounds each. Men blasphemed God because of the plague of the hail, since that plague was exceedingly great—Revelation 16:1–21.
- John is shown—in detail—the destruction of Babylon and exactly how Babylon receives the "Fierceness of the Wrath of God." In Babylon was found the blood of the prophets and saints and of all who were slain on earth. God repays Babylon double. Babylon is made desolate and shall not be found anymore. This destruction of Babylon will fulfill many Old Testament prophecies. Babylon is fallen, is fallen! Strong is the Lord God who judges Babylon—Revelation 17:1–19:10.

- The Battle of Armageddon—Jesus is victorious—Revelation 19:11–20:3.
- The Antichrist and the False Prophet are thrown alive into the Lake of Fire—Revelation 19:11–20:3.
- The rest are killed with the sword that proceeds from the mouth of Jesus [the Word of God] —Revelation 19:11–20:3.
- Satan is bound and is thrown into a bottomless pit for 1,000 years—Revelation 19:11–20:3.
- This is the end of the "Wrath of God"—which will last approximately 965 days—almost three years—Daniel 12:4-13; Revelation 19:11–20:3.
- We can understand this, because on day 2,300—in other words, two thousand three hundred days after the Antichrist has Stopped the Daily Sacrifices at the Temple—the Sanctuary [the Temple] will be cleansed [The Temple will be cleansed]. This would certainly happen when Jesus begins to rule the earth for 1,000 years from Jerusalem. This event—when the Temple will be cleansed—will occur after the Battle of Armageddon is over—after Satan is cast into the bottomless pit. When we subtract 1,335 from 2,300, we can understand that the "Wrath of God" will last approximately 965 days—almost three years—Daniel 12:4-13.
- Jesus begins to rule the earth for 1,000 years from Jerusalem—Revelation 20:4–10.
- Jesus rules the world with a rod of iron—Revelation 20:4–10.
- Christians live and reign with Jesus—as Kings and Priests—during this 1,000-year period—Revelation 20:4–10.
- When the 1,000 years have expired, Satan is released from the bottomless pit—Revelation 20:4–10.
- Satan goes out to deceive all the nations and is able to deceive many people who choose to follow Satan instead of Jesus—Revelation 20:4–10.
- Satan gathers an army for battle—whose number is as the sand of the sea—Revelation 20:4–10.
- Satan and his army surround Jerusalem and prepare to attack Jesus—Revelation 20:4–10.
- Fire comes down from God and devours Satan and his army—Revelation 20:4–10.

- Satan is cast into the Lake of Fire, where the Antichrist and the False Prophet are—Revelation 20:4–10.
- Satan and the Antichrist and the False Prophet are tormented day and night forever—in the Lake of Fire—Revelation 20:4–10.
- The "Great White Throne" Judgment. All the unsaved dead are judged according to their works—Revelation 20:11–15.
- Anyone whose name is not found written in the Book of Life is cast into the Lake of Fire—Revelation 20:11–15.
- All of the unsaved dead are cast into the Lake of Fire—Revelation 20:11–15.
- Death and Hades are cast into the Lake of Fire—Revelation 20:11–15.
- The Lake of Fire is the Second Death—Revelation 20:11–15.
- Only those whose names are written in the Book of Life are allowed to enter the "New Jerusalem"—Revelation 21:1–22:21.
- There is a "New Heaven" and a "New Earth"—Revelation 21:1–22:21.

Please understand:
My Job is NOT to convince you that the Bible is True.
My Job is to Teach you What the Bible Says.
It is the Holy Spirit's Job to convince you that the Bible is True.

Jesus instructs His disciples to "Stand" and to "Overcome" and to be "Faithful unto Death". Therefore, it is important for a disciple of Jesus to understand this Bible Truth:

TRIBULATION and **PERSECUTION**
come from our **STAND**
on the **WORD of GOD** and our **TESTIMONY of JESUS**.

Even so, come, Lord Jesus.

Printed in the USA
CPSIA information can be obtained
at www.ICGtesting.com
CBHW050440210124
3567CB00005B/15